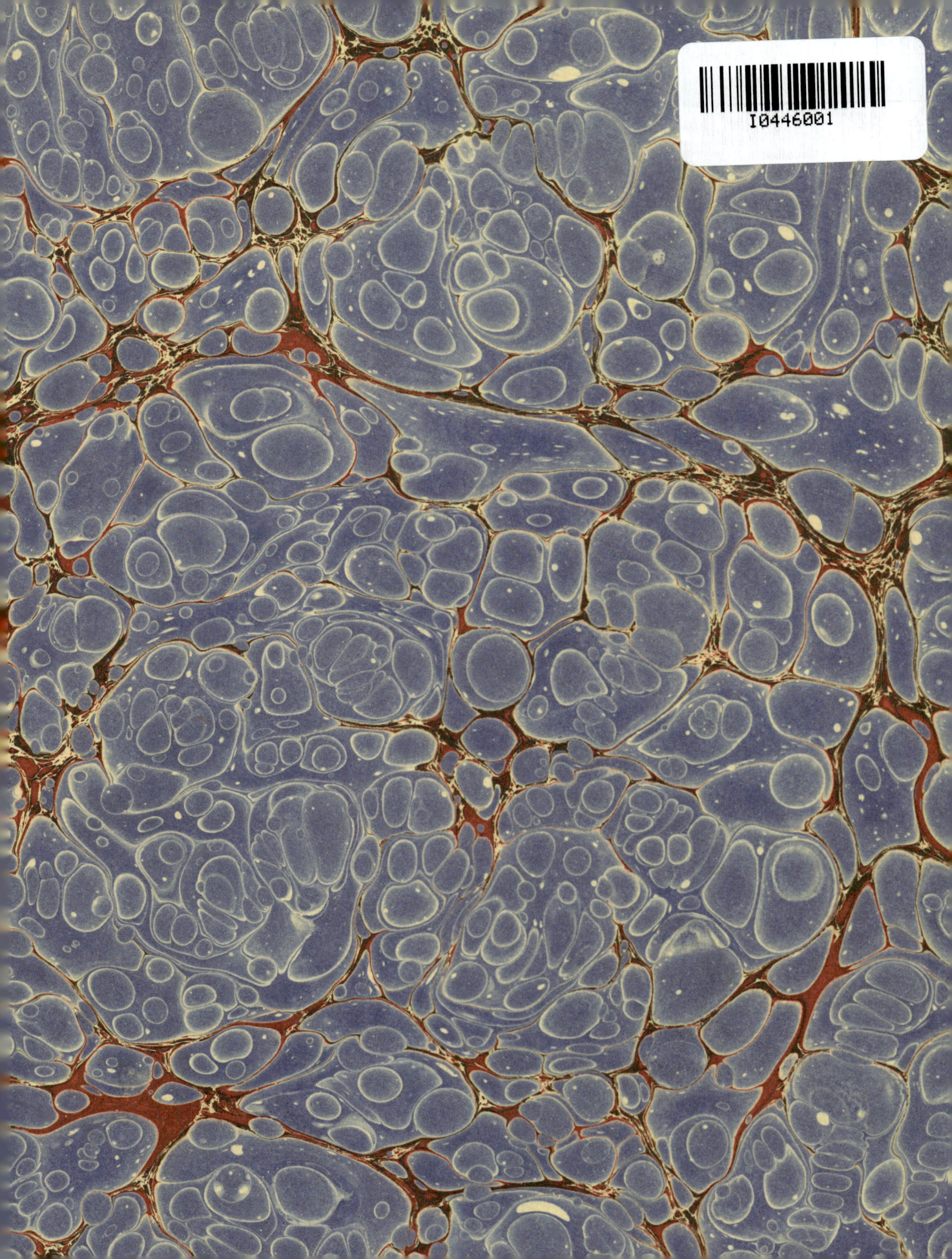

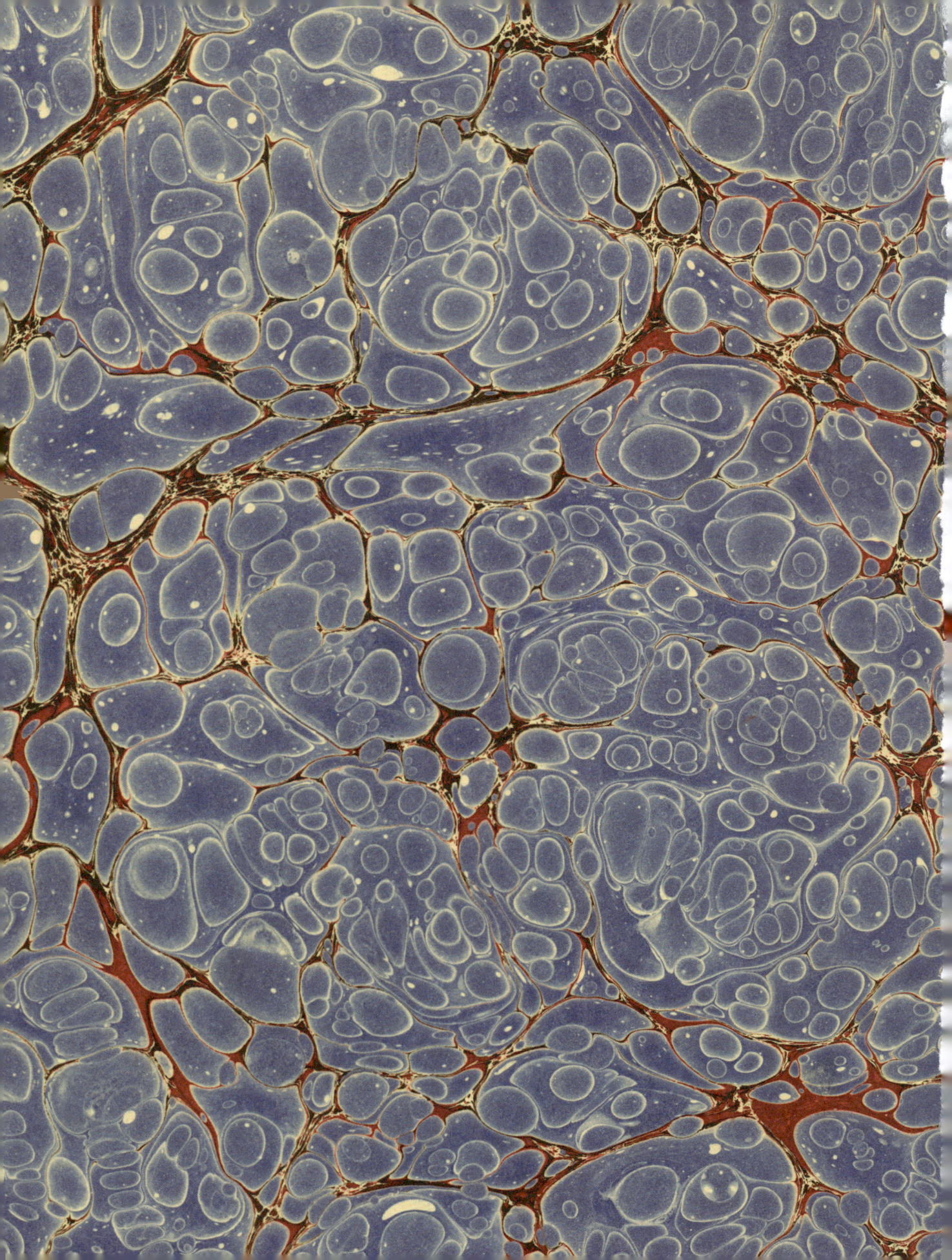

Every year, the fashion industry is responsible for more greenhouse gas emissions than all international flights and container ships combined.

Photographs of British Algae: Cyanotype Imperfections

Photographs of British Algae:
Cyanotype Imperfections

Mandy Barker

GOST

Waterproof material

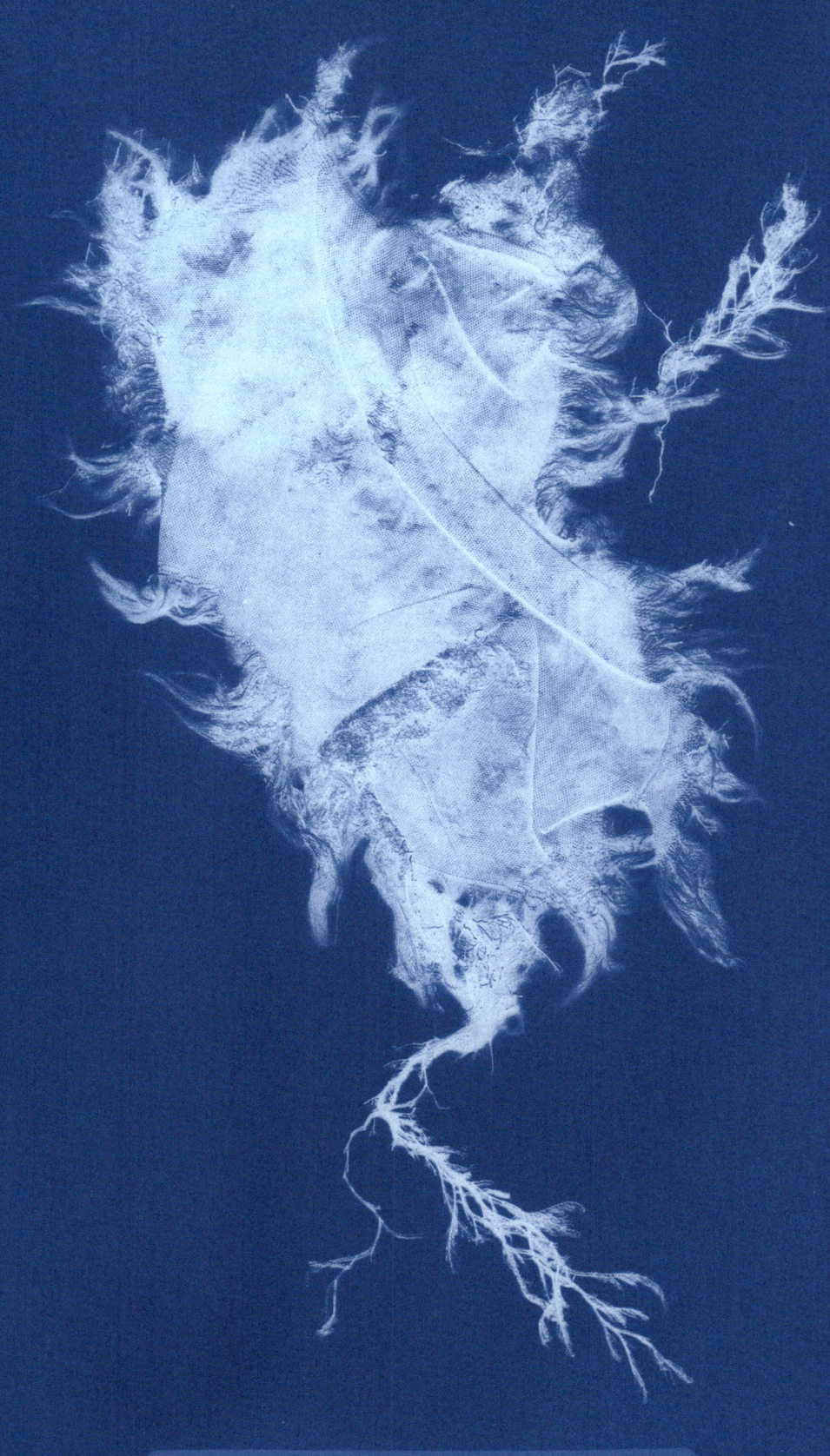

Fucus imperviös. var. irrigö.

High-visibility jacket

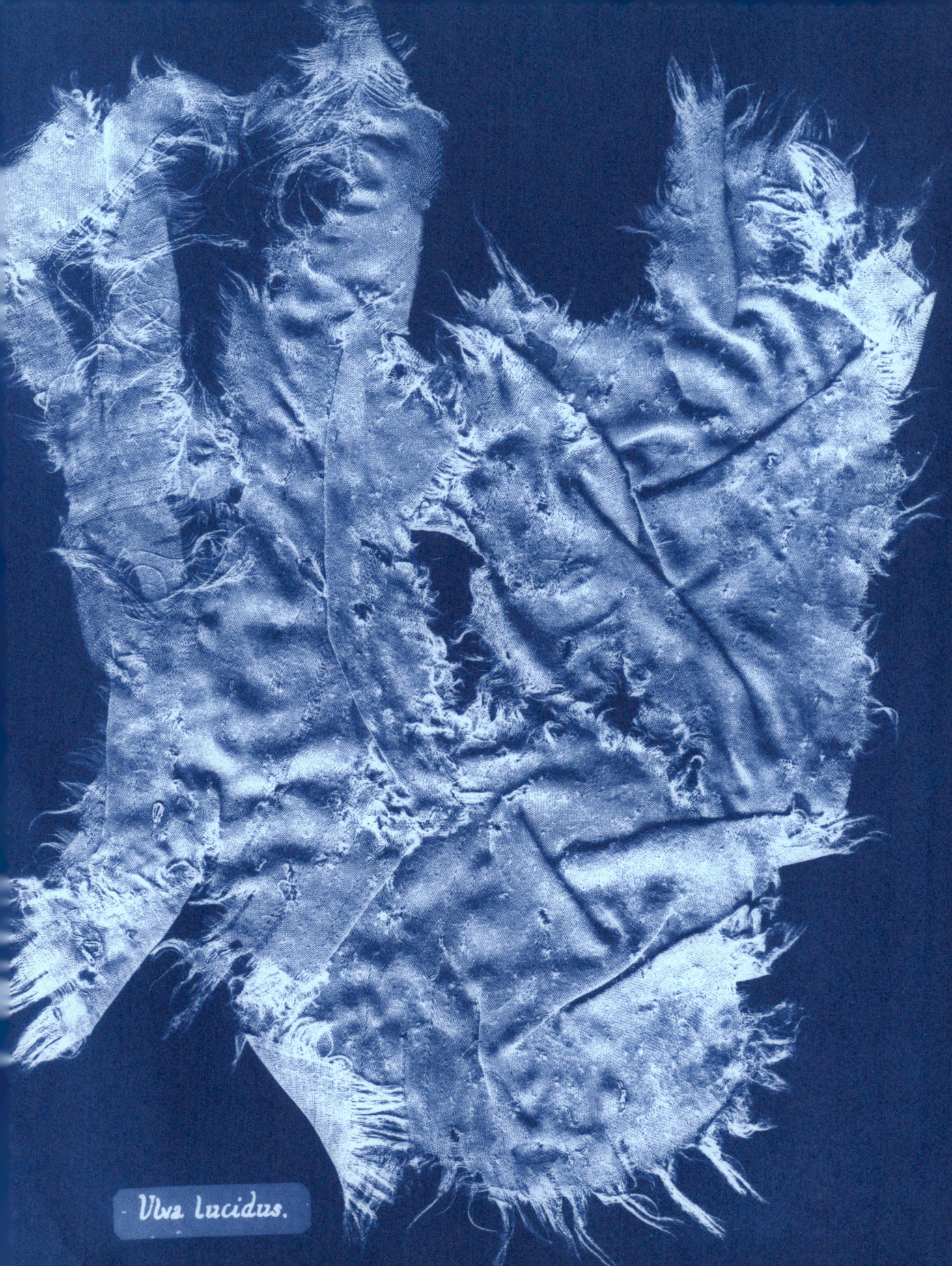

Ulva lucidus.

Cagoule

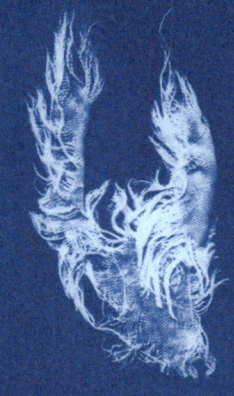

Calothrix impervious.

Parka

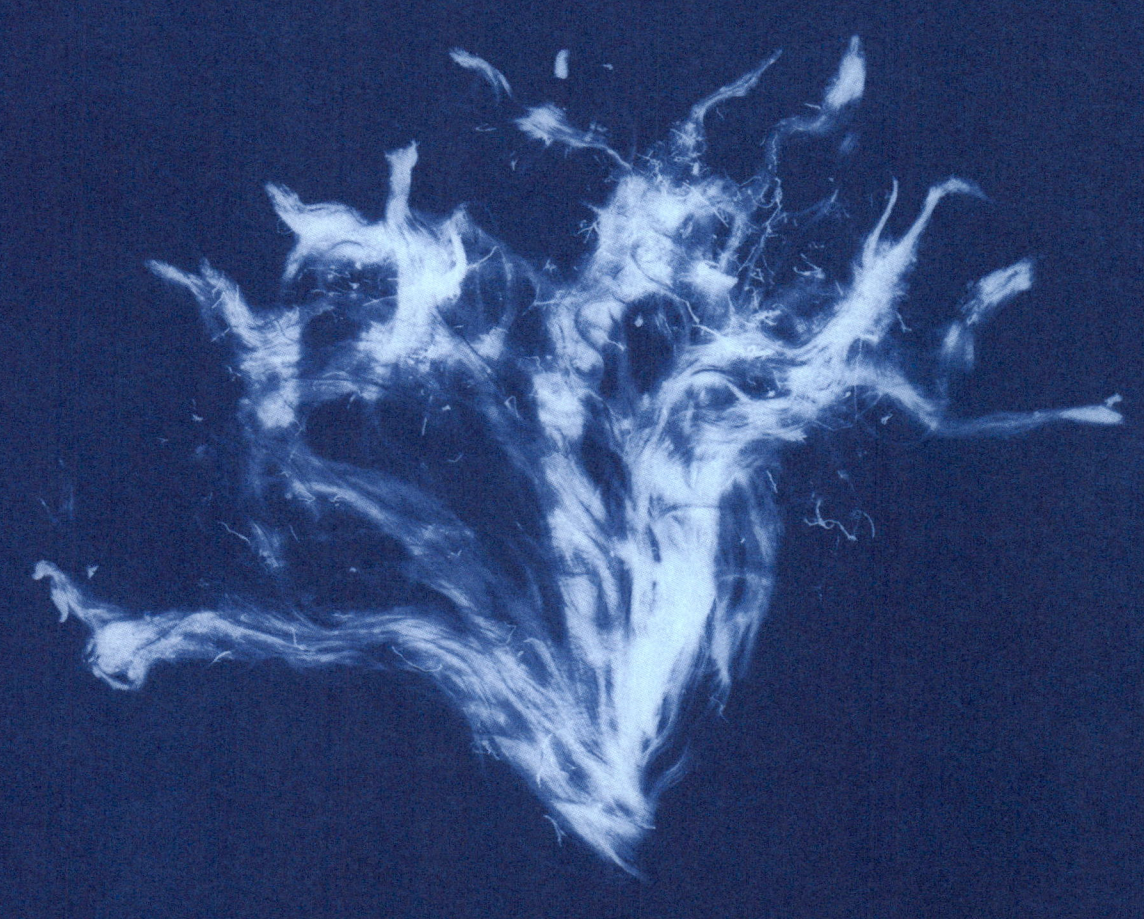

Ectocarpus fictus

Bomber jacket

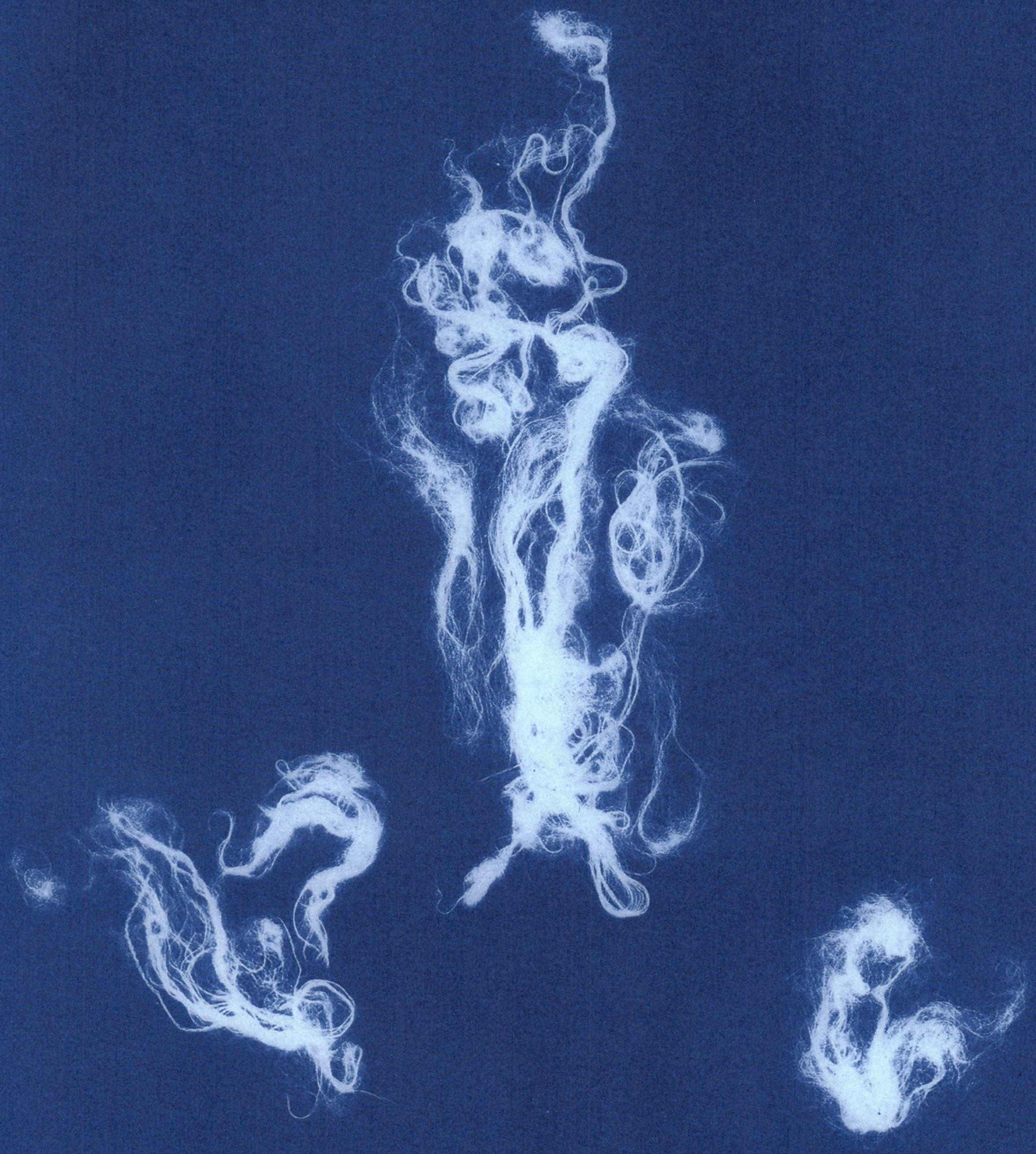

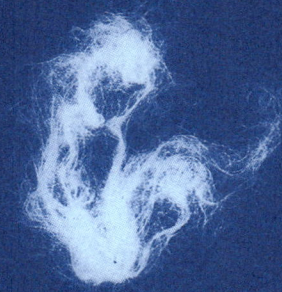

Lyngbya filum.

Coat lining

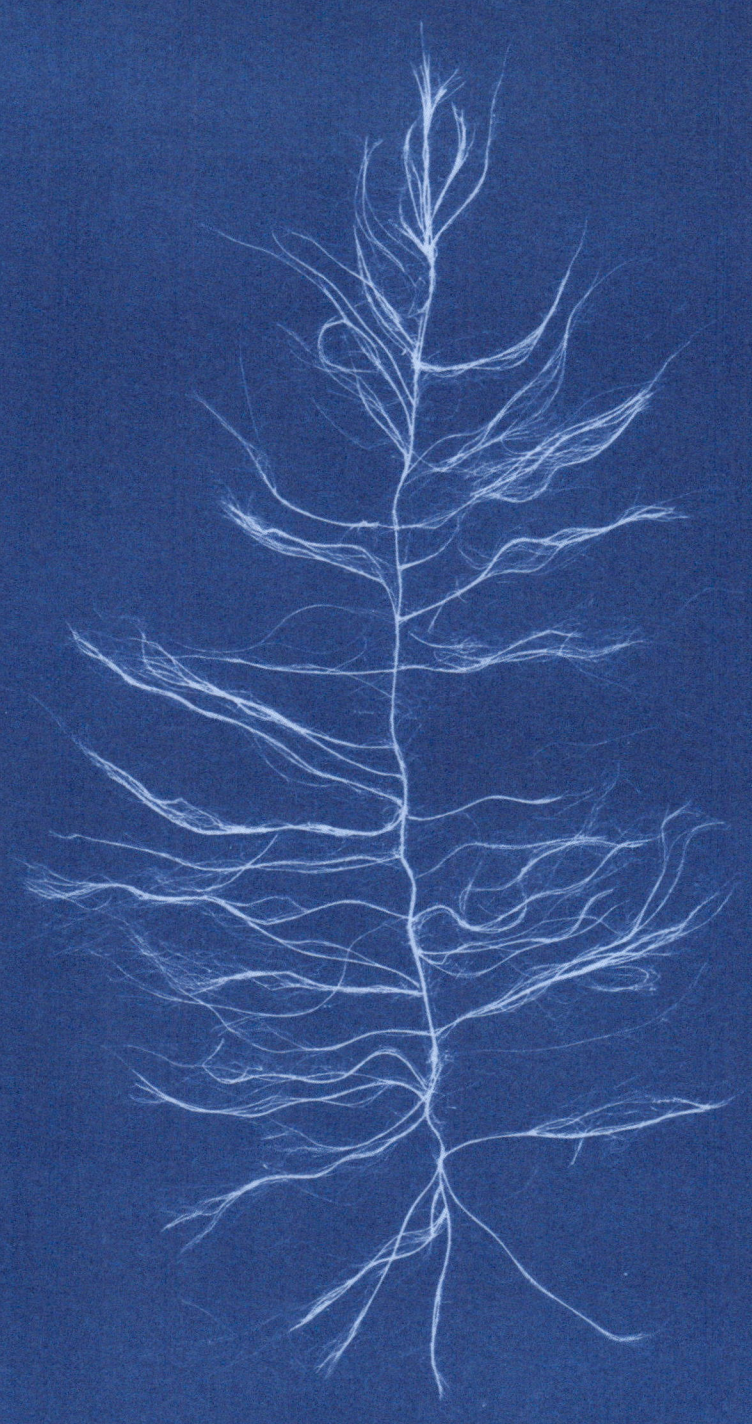

Dichloria vestis.

Jacket lining

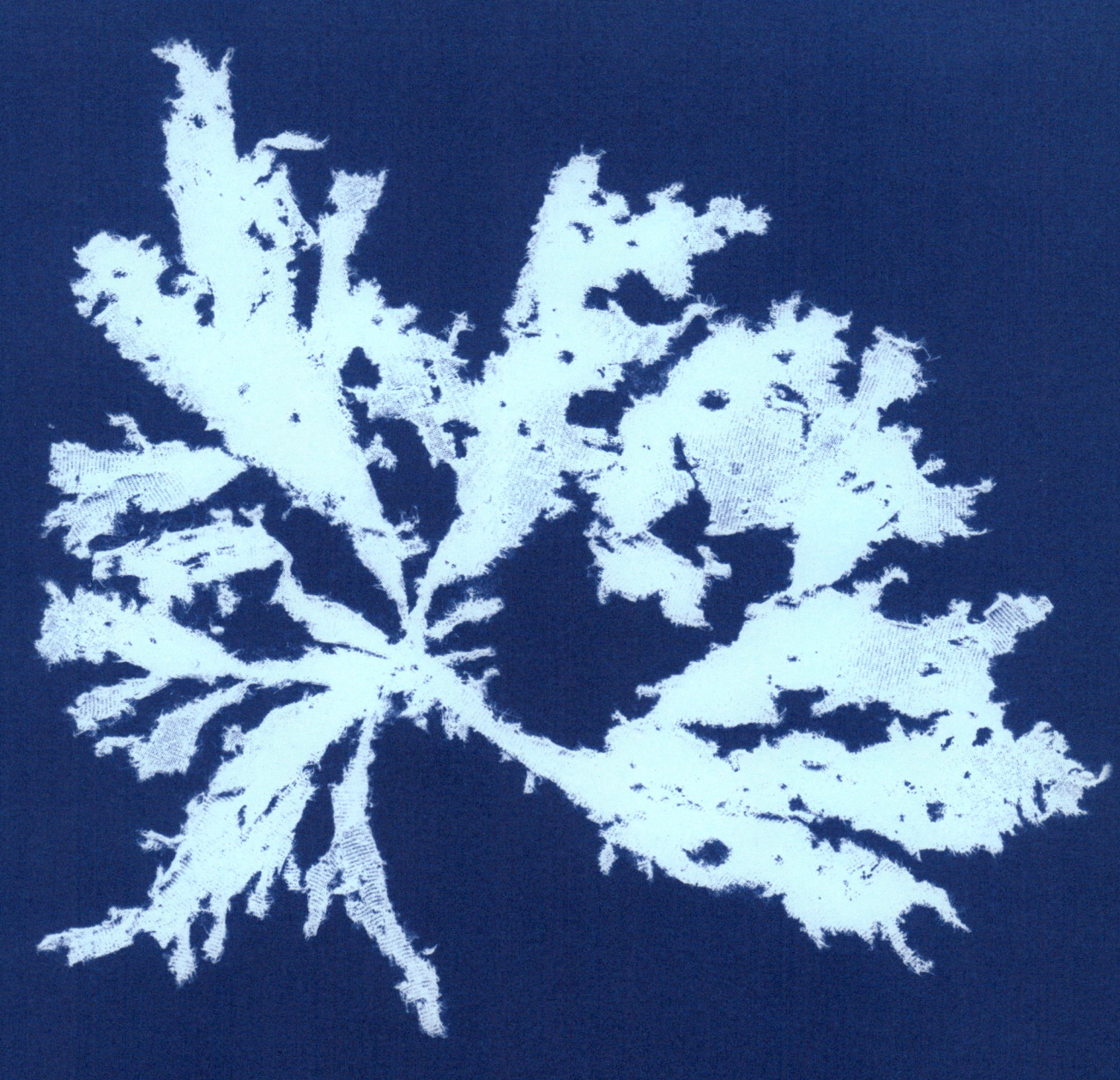

Rhodomenia ignotus

School uniform jumper

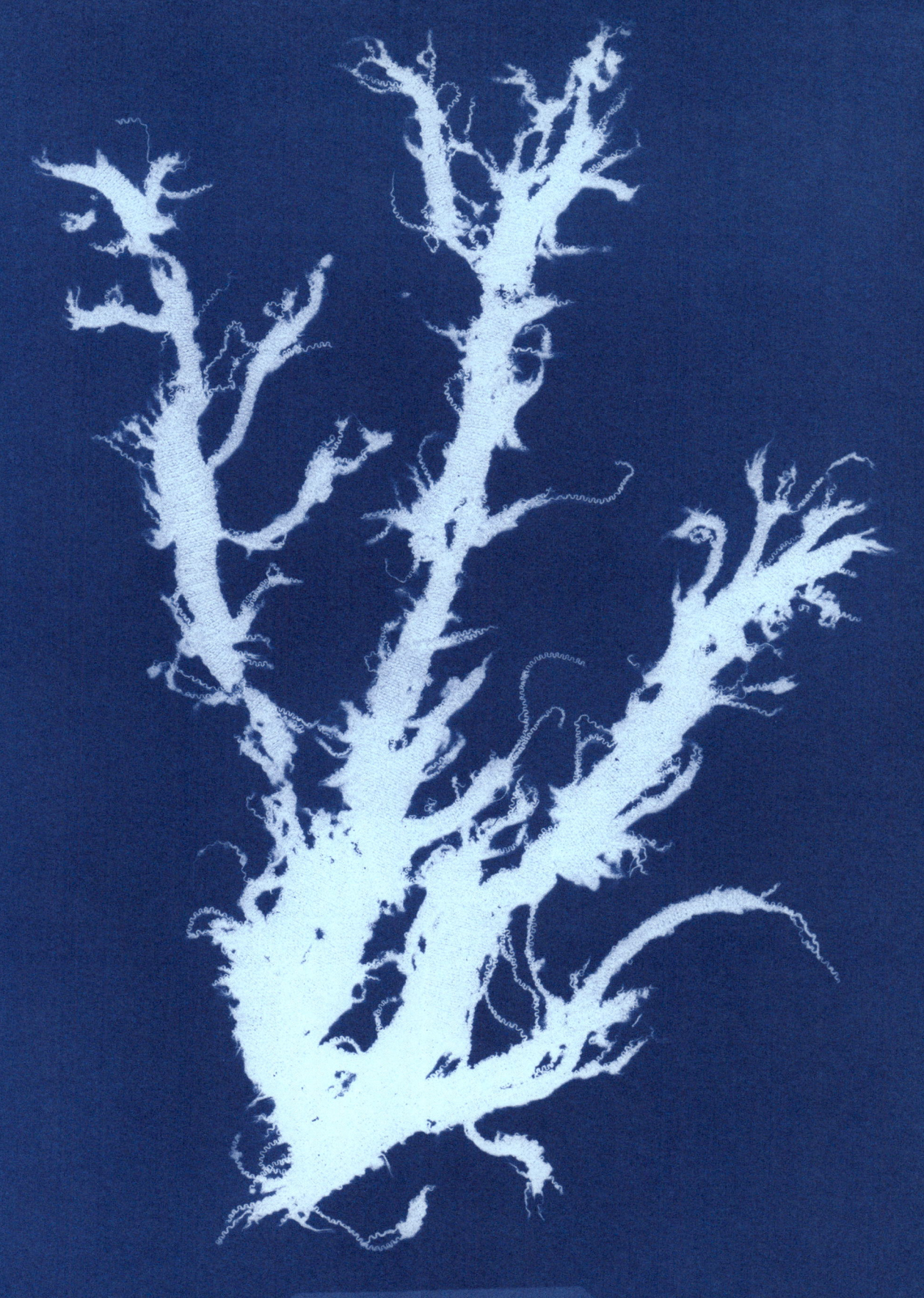

Halydrys schola.

Sweater

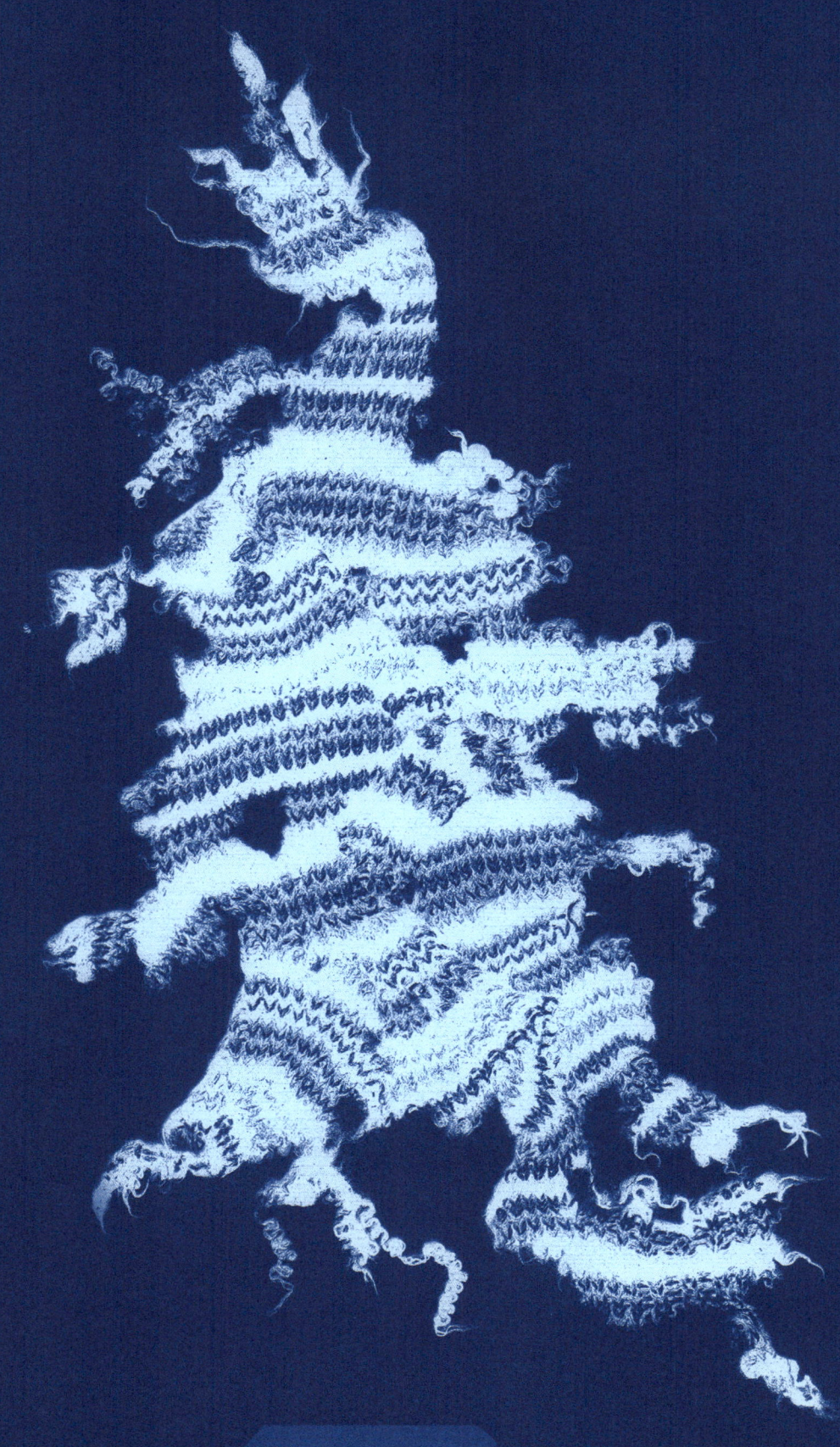

Conferva sūdō.

Cardigan

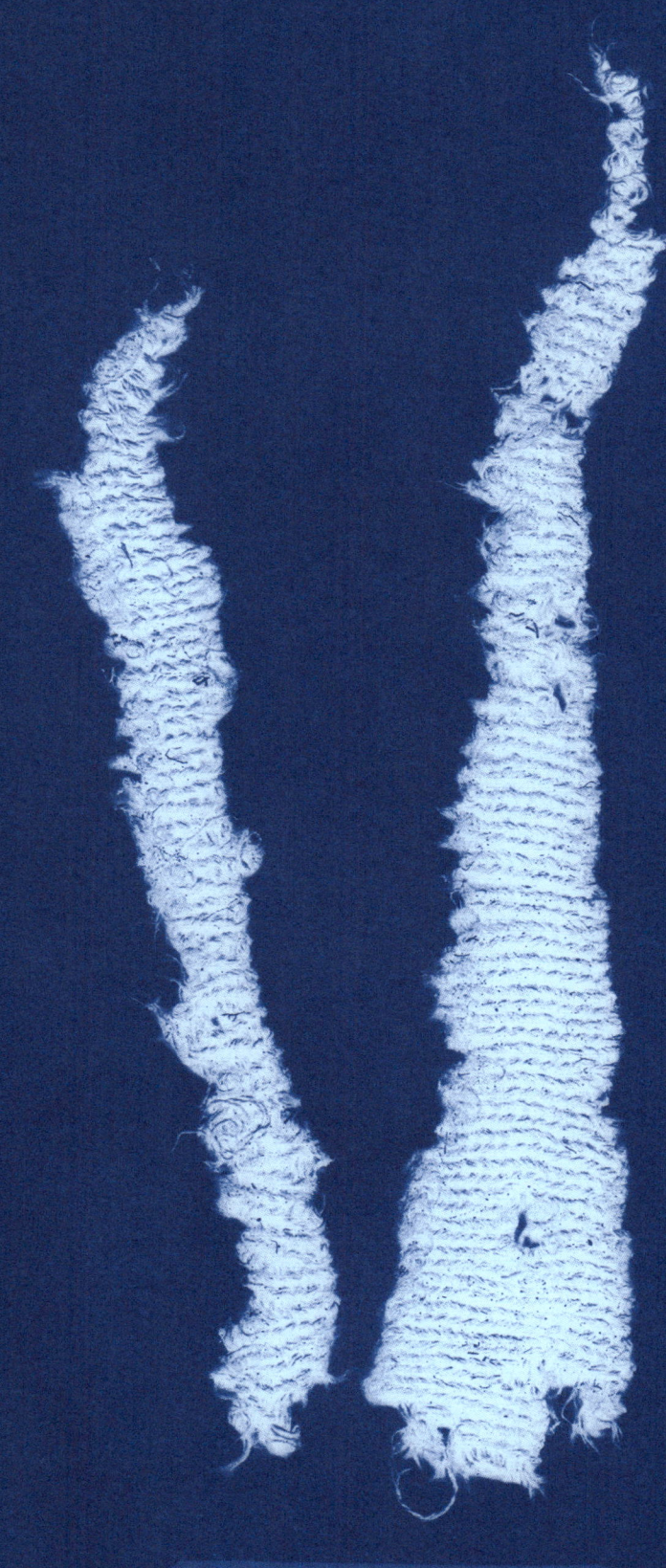

Laminaria cursus.

Tank top

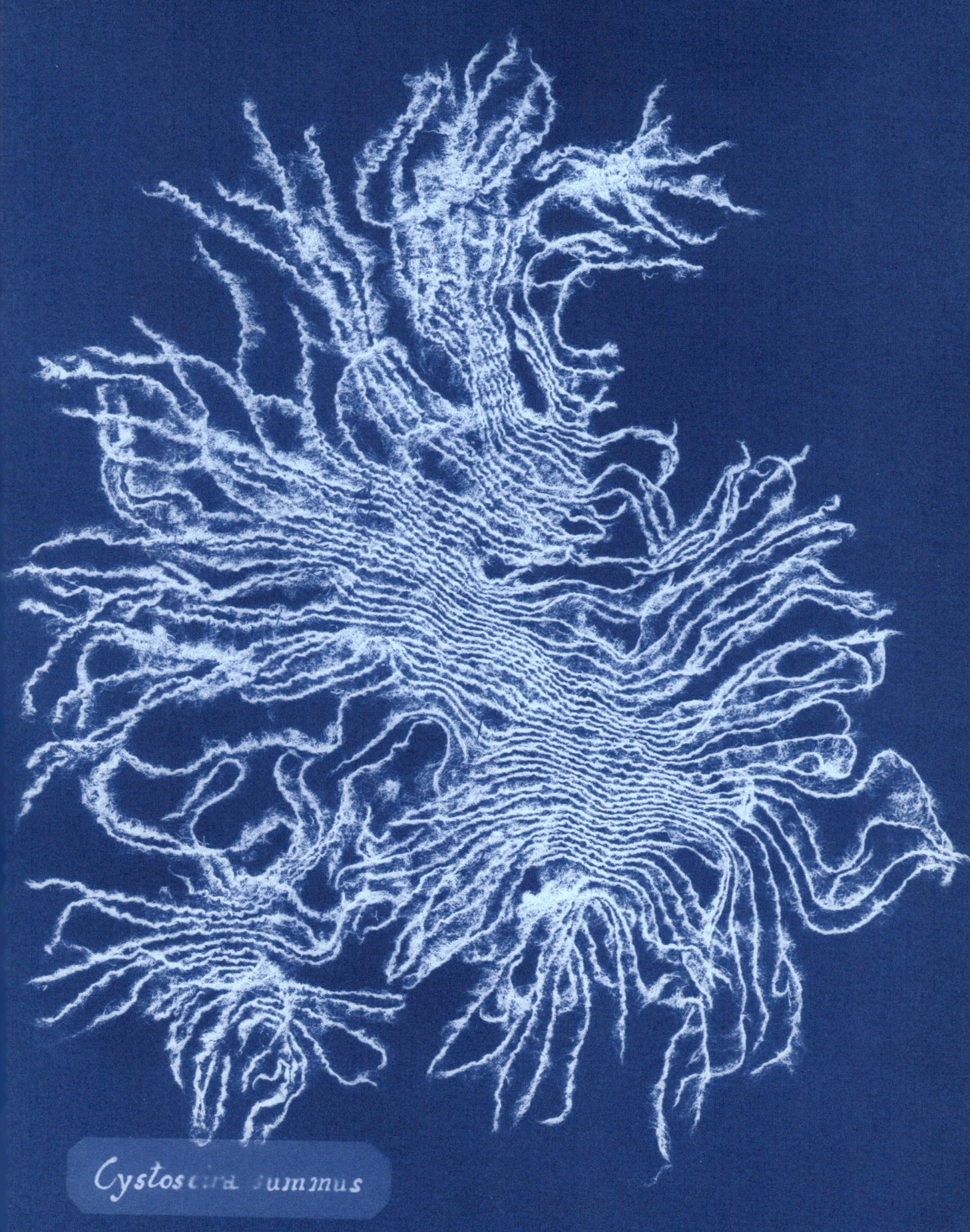

Cystoseira summus

Fine knit cardigan

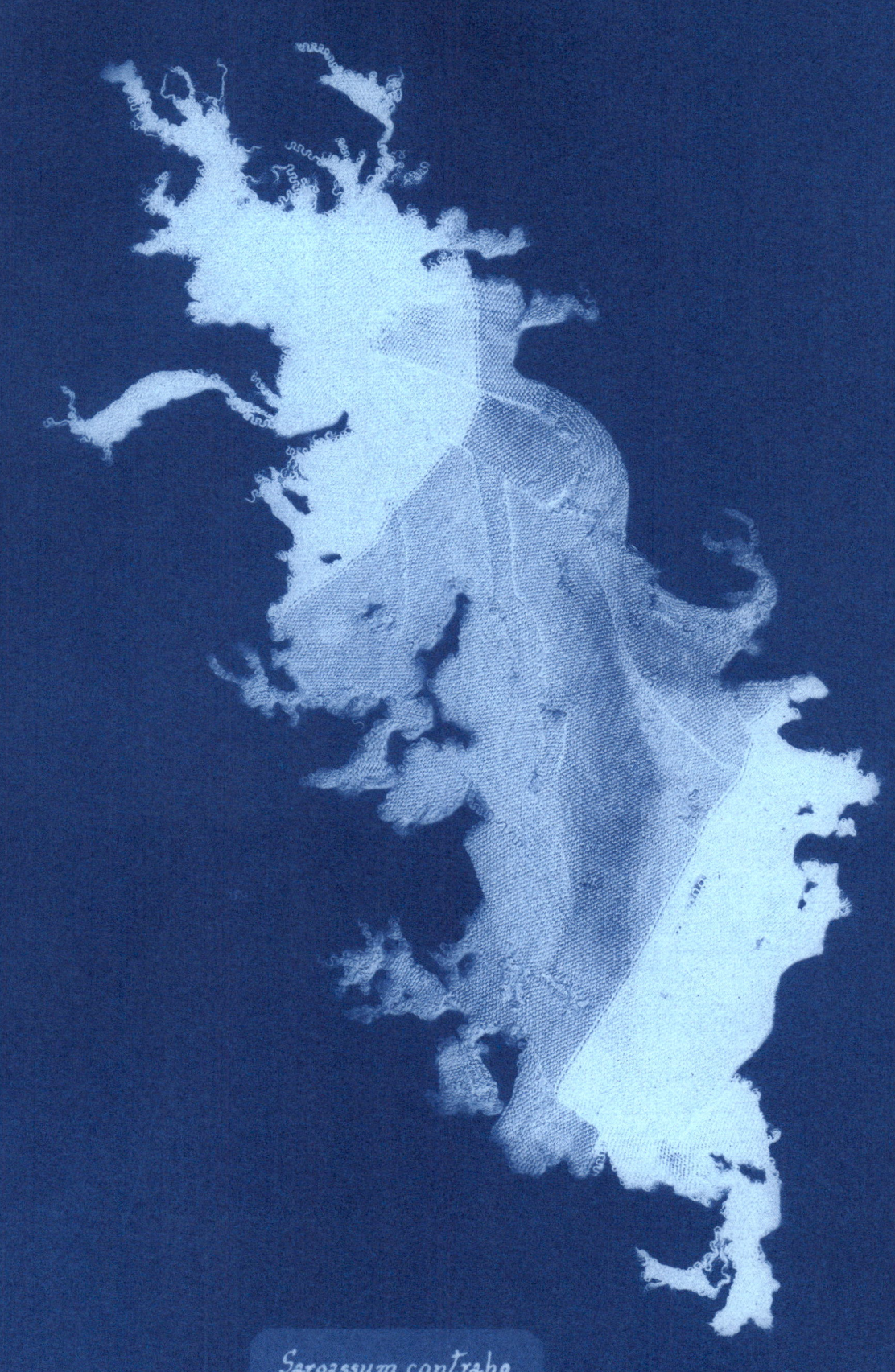

Sargassum contraho.

Shawl

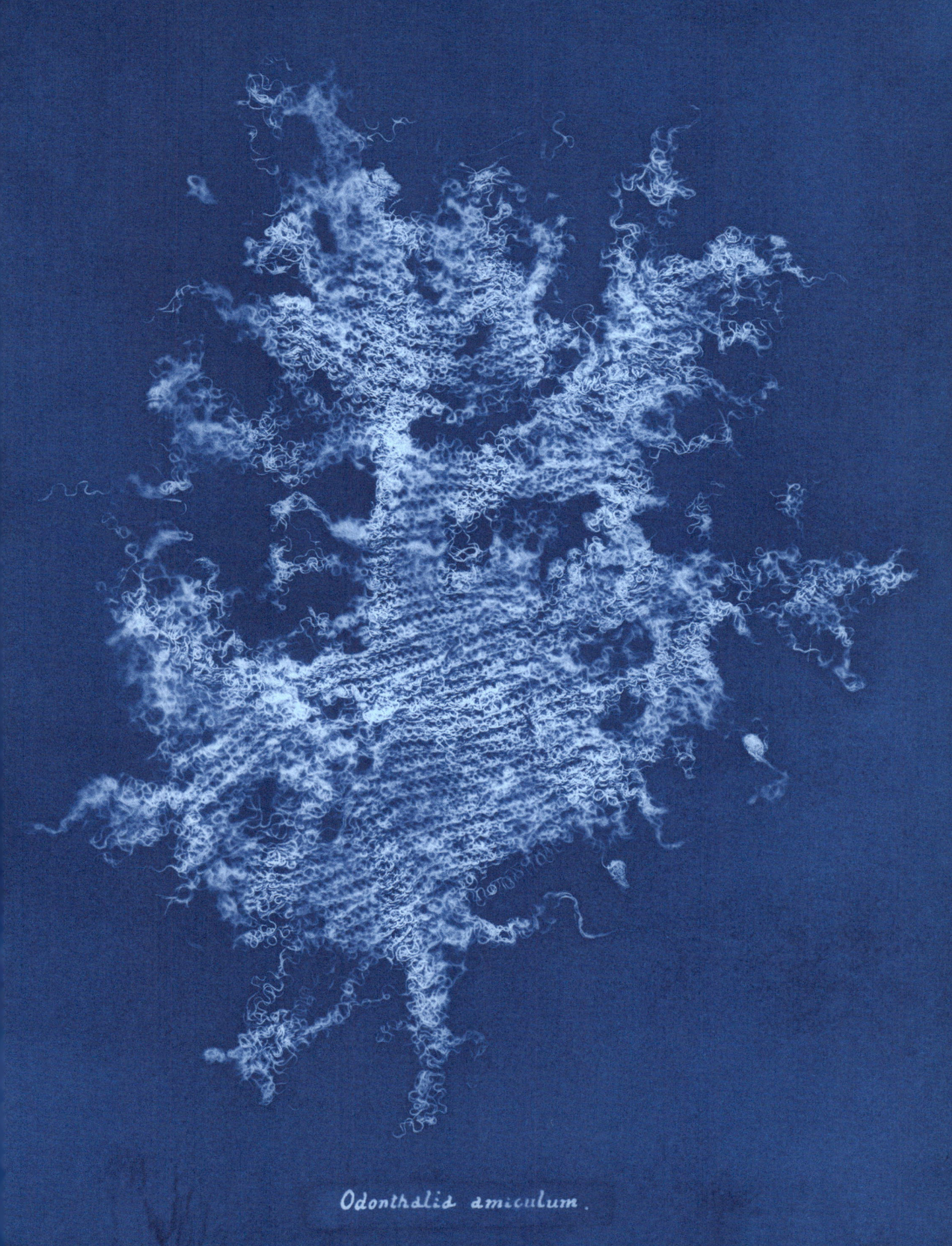

Odonthalia amiculum.

Lining (with algae)

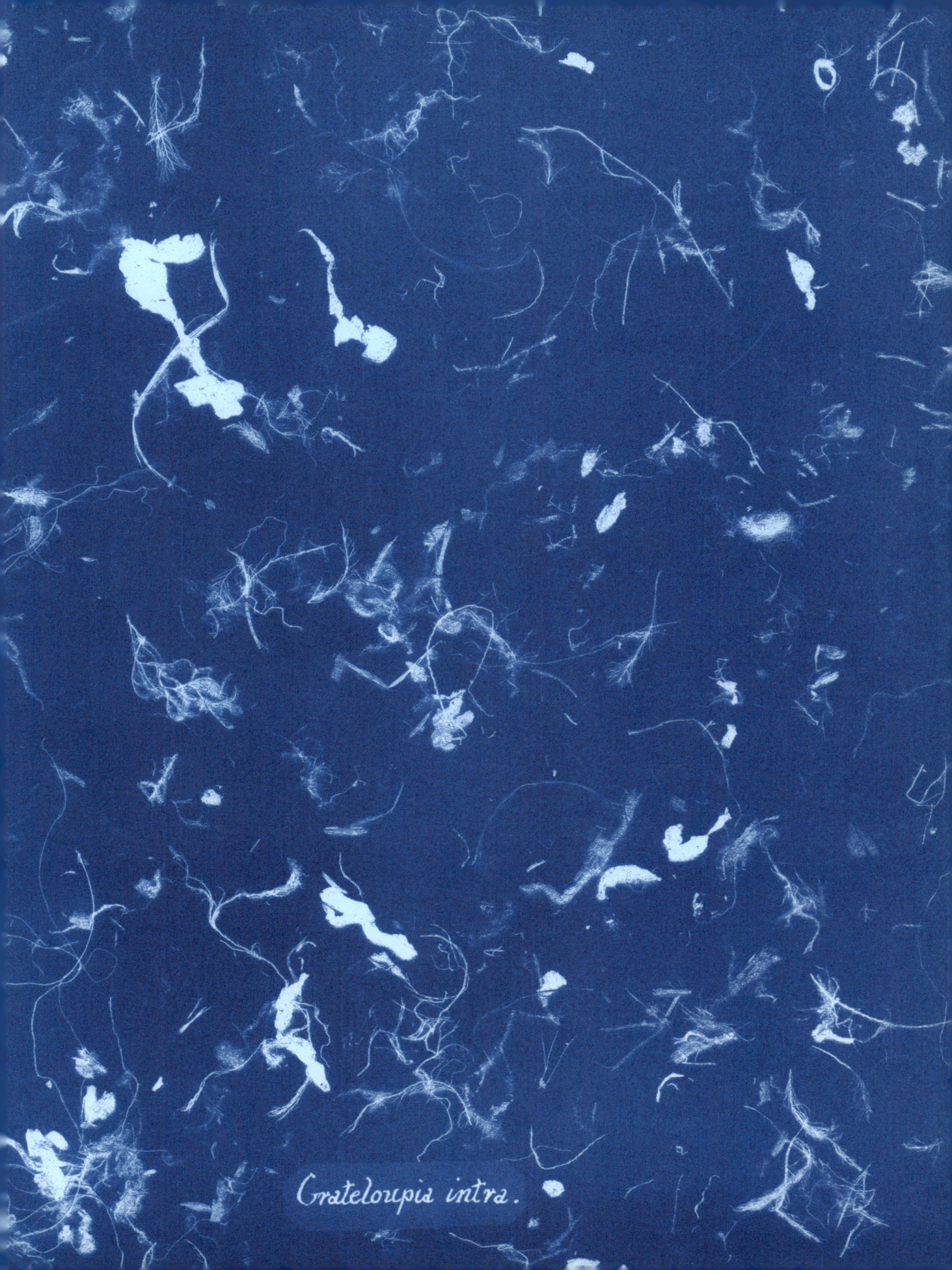

Grateloupia intra.

Trousers

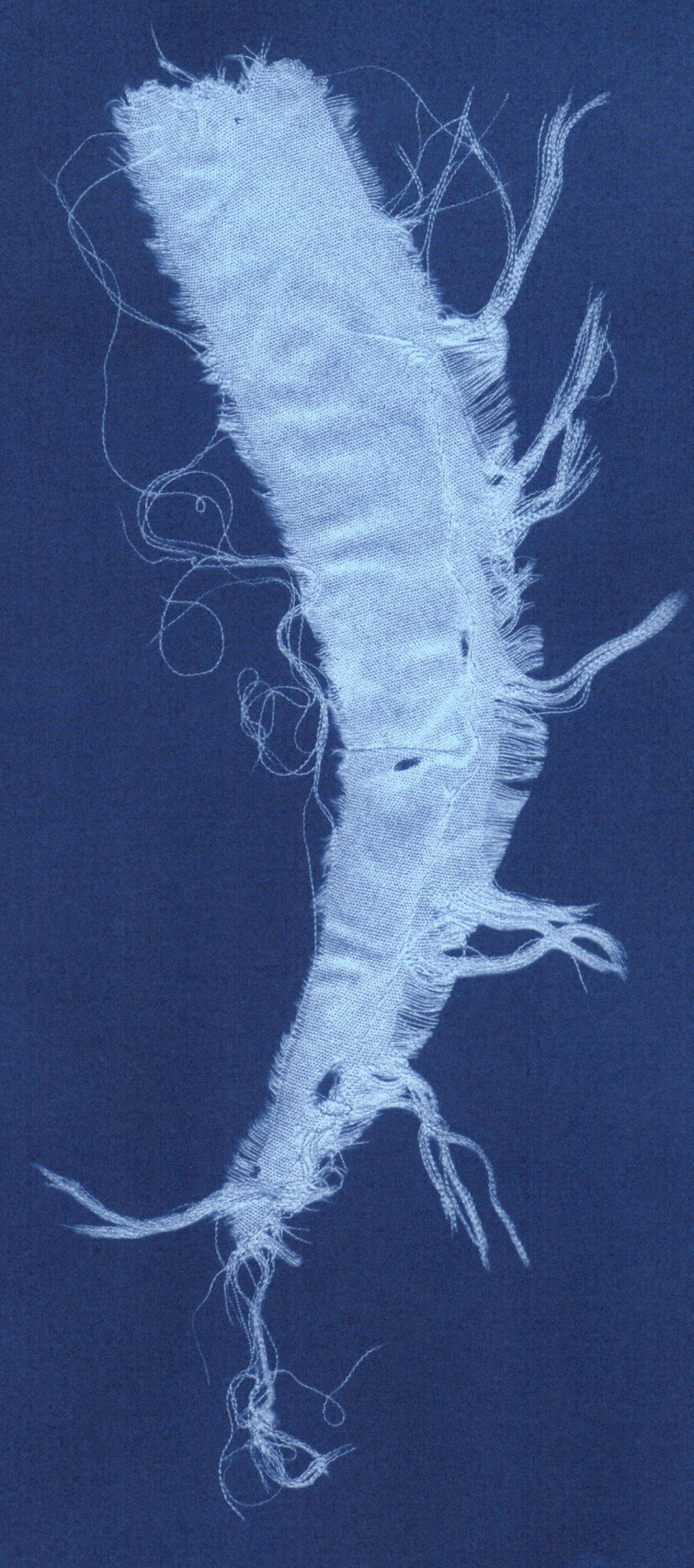

Rhodomenia feminalia.

Trouser pocket

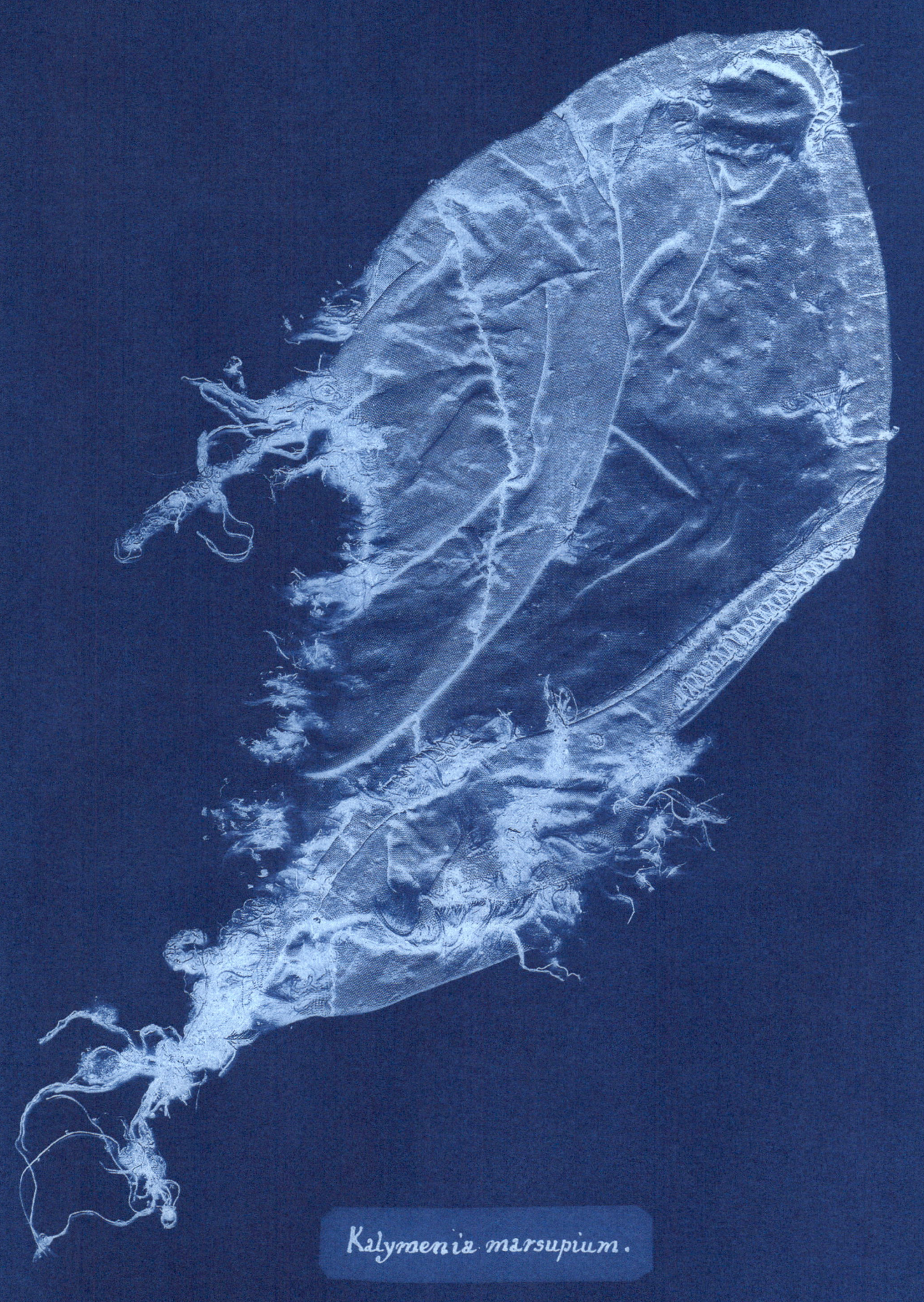

Kalymenia marsupium.

Jogging bottoms

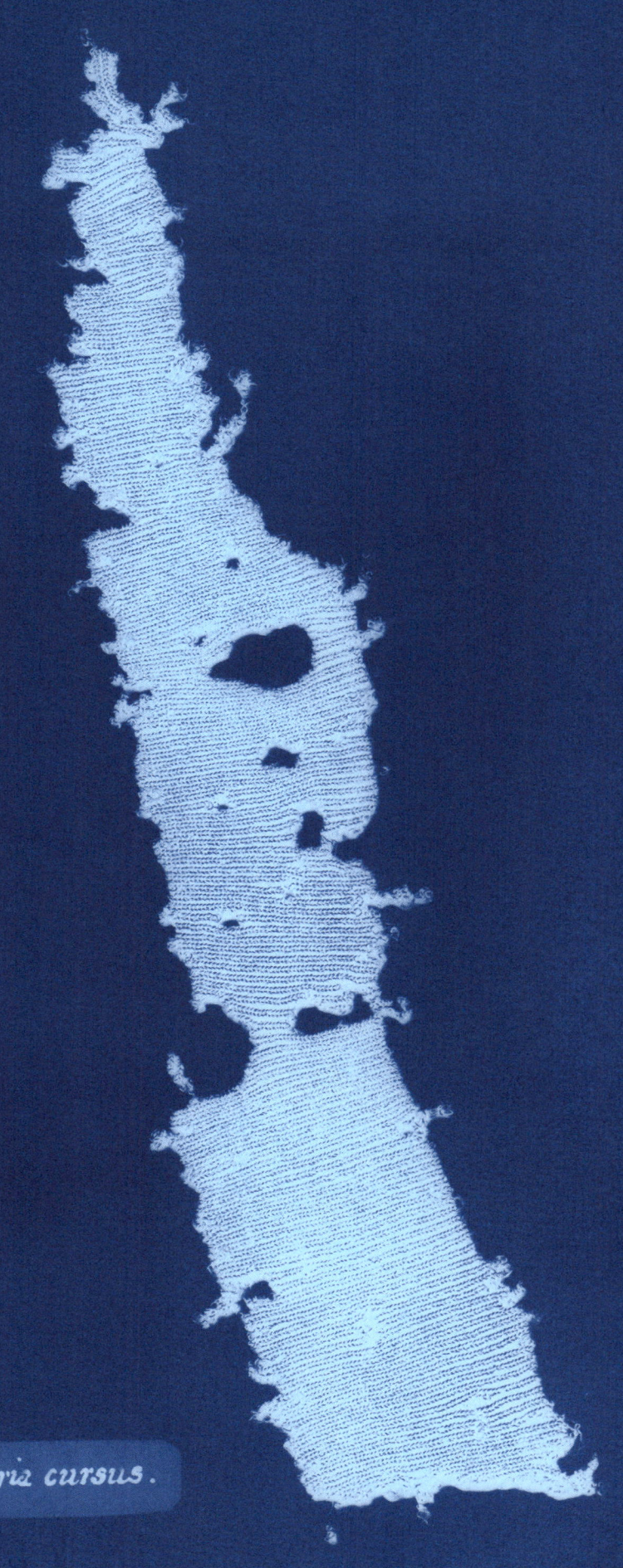

Punctaria cursus.

Dress

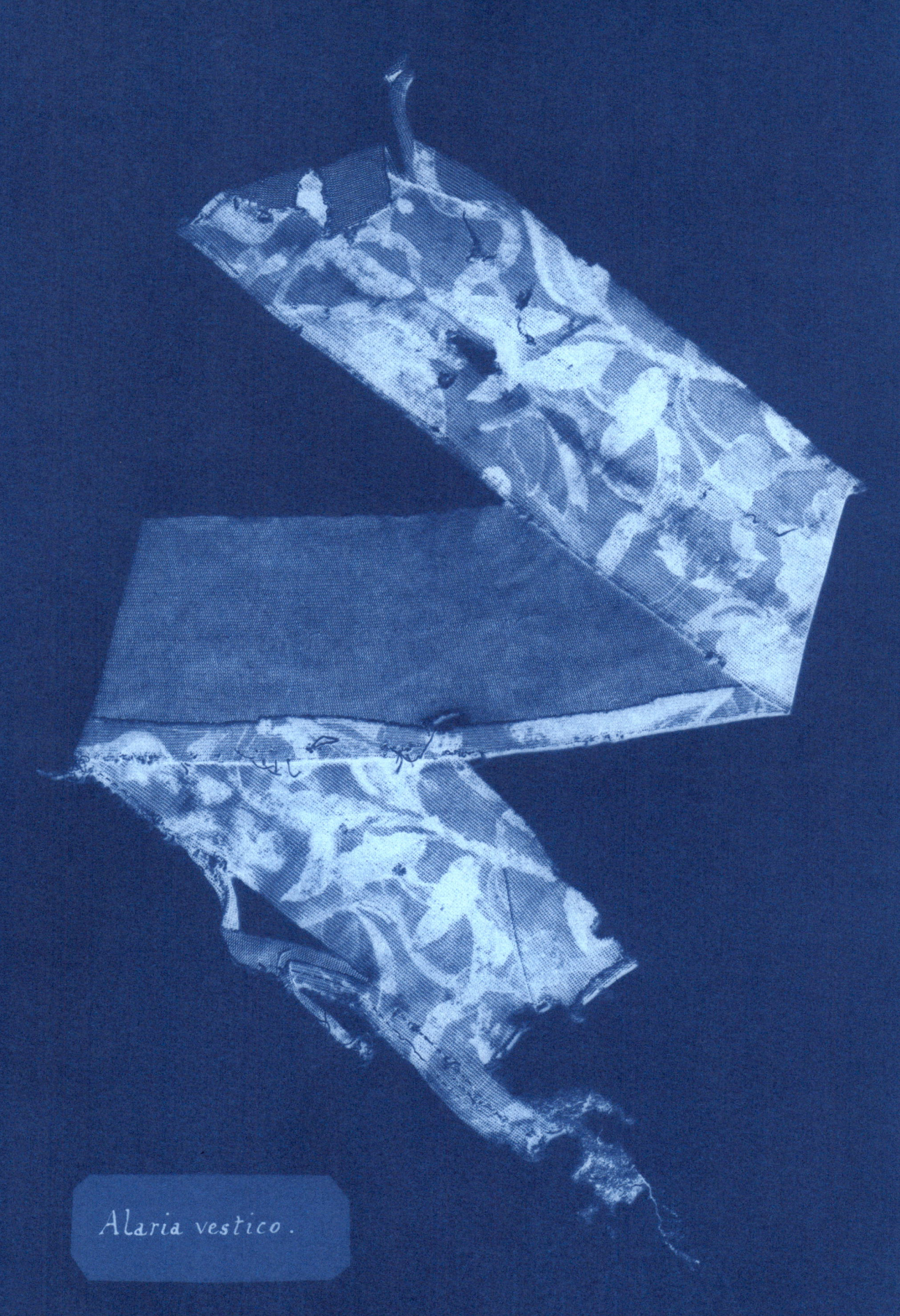

Alaria vestico.

Waistband (with algae)

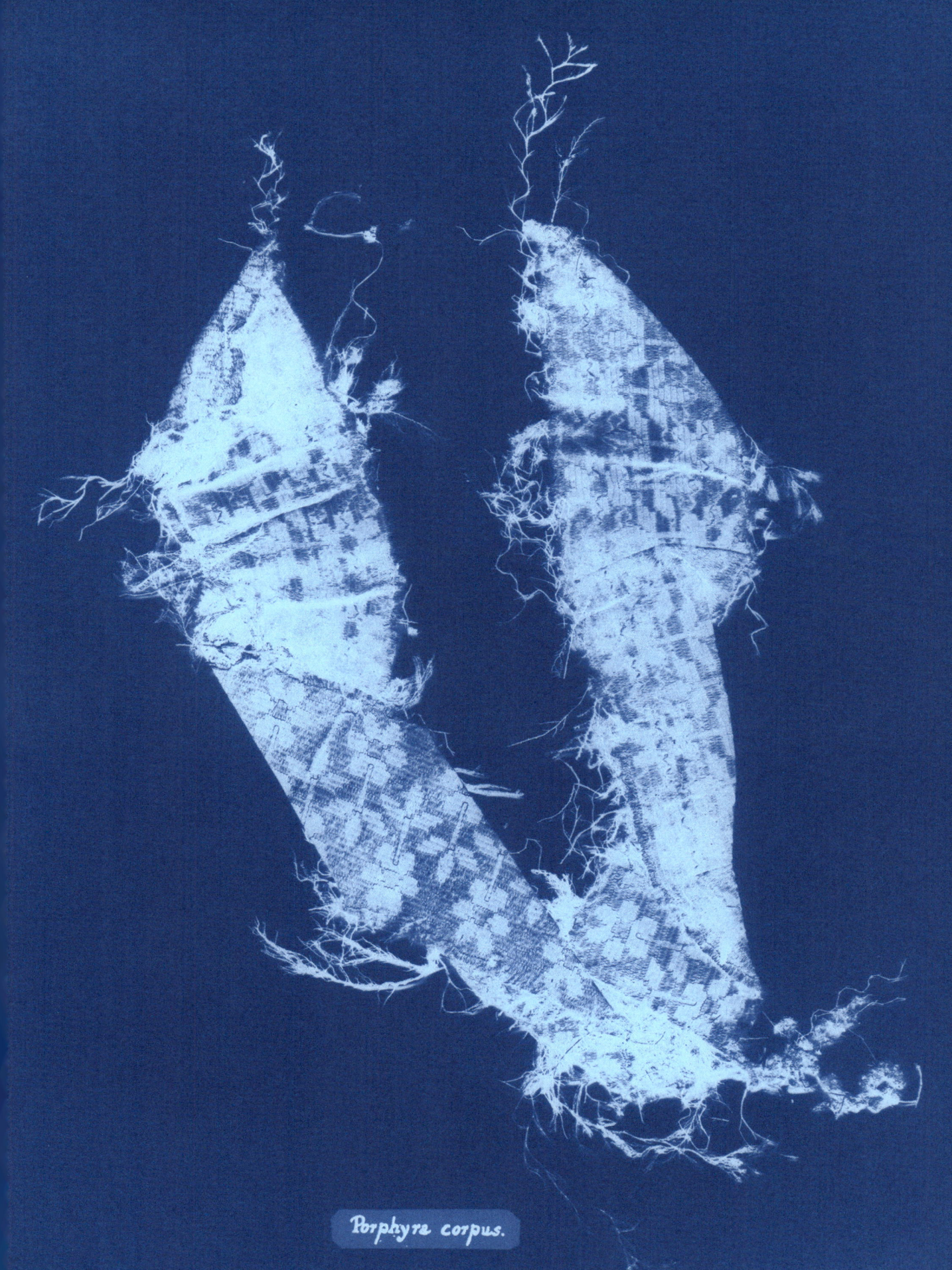

Porphyra corpus.

Waistband

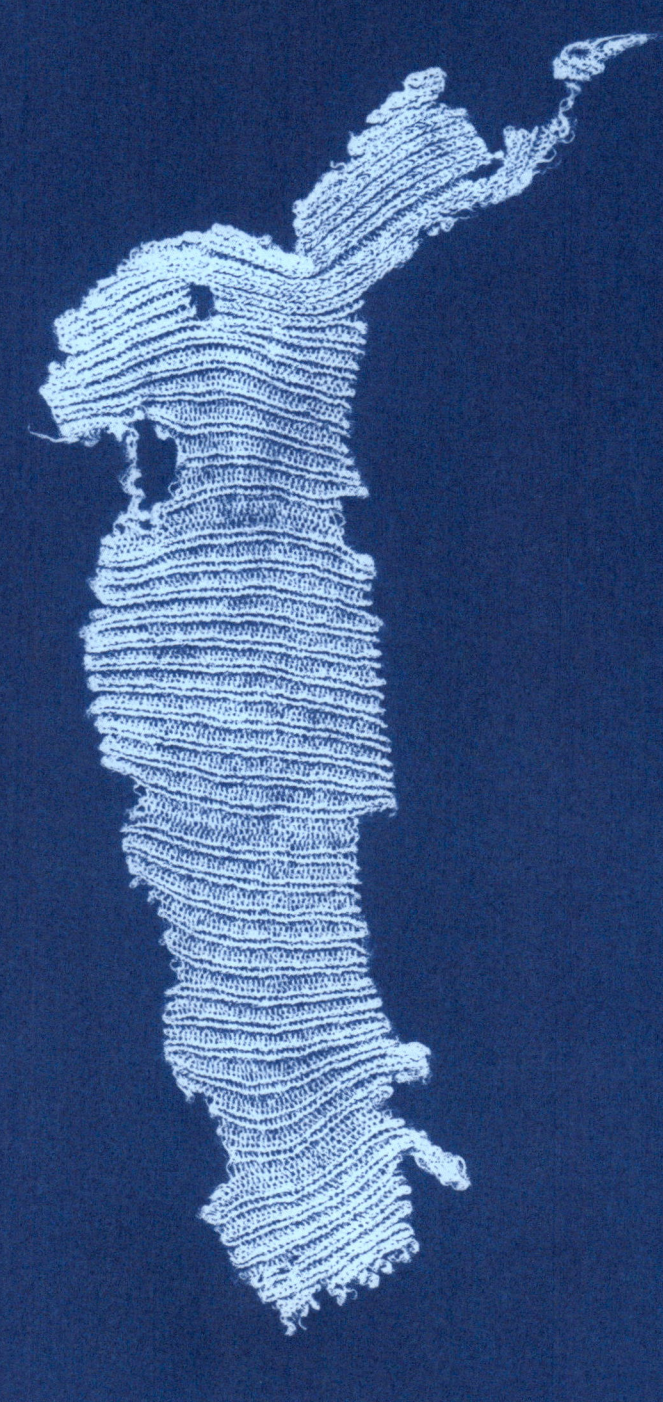

Ulva corpus.

Patterned blouse

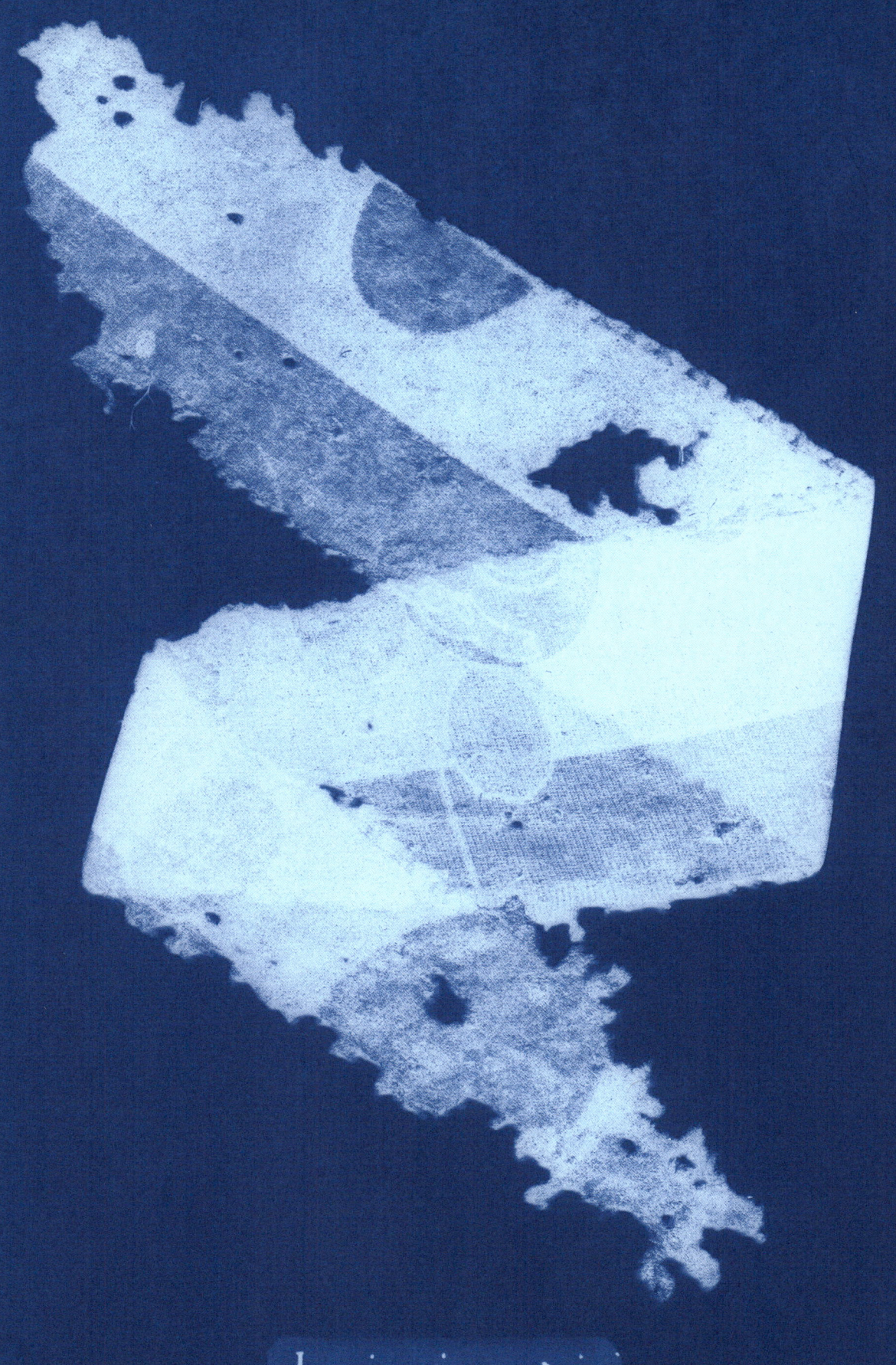

Laminaria materia

Floral blouse

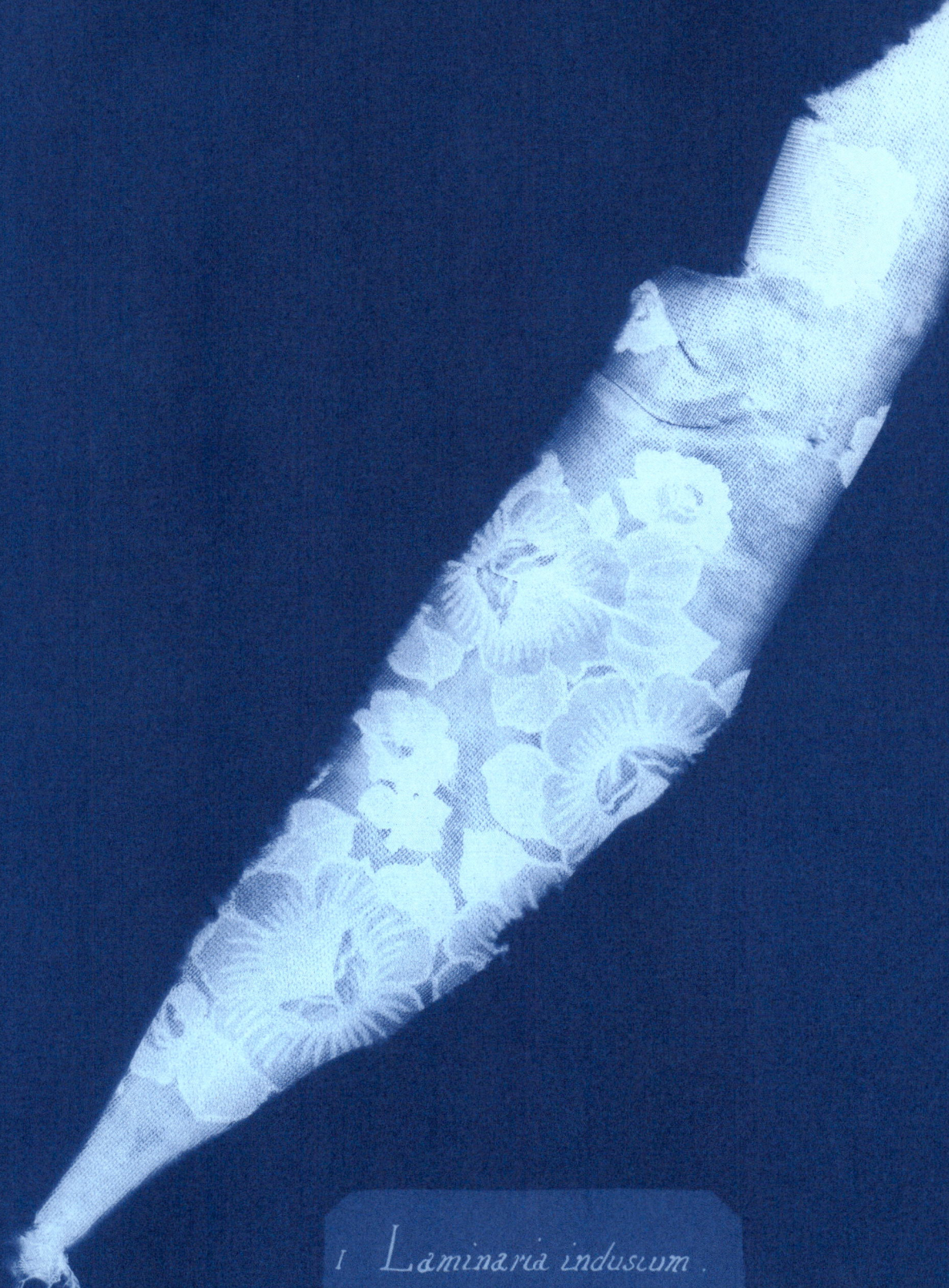

1 *Laminaria indusium.*

Synthetic satin blouse

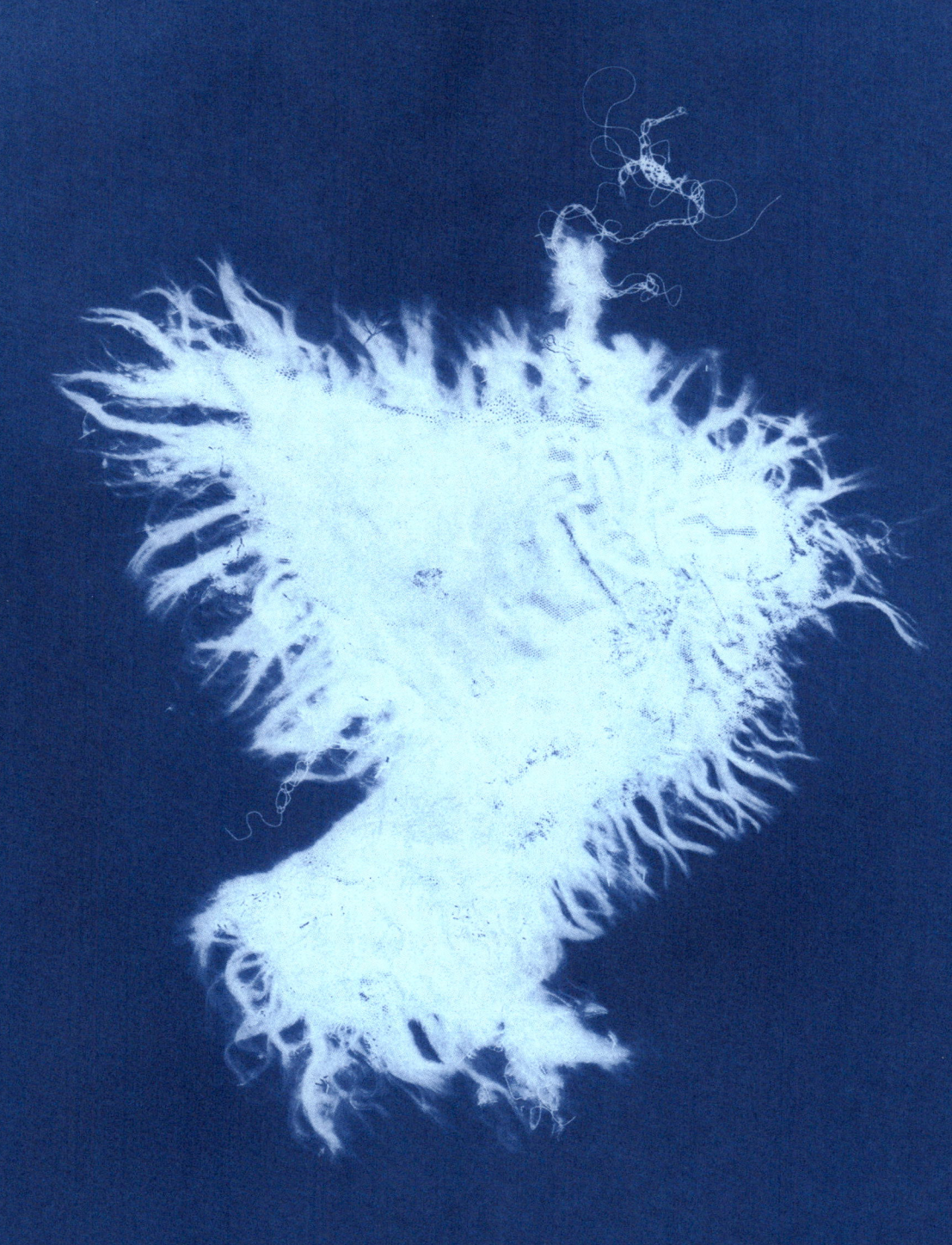

Zygnema sutum.

Two blouses

Asperococcus indusium

Shirt cuff

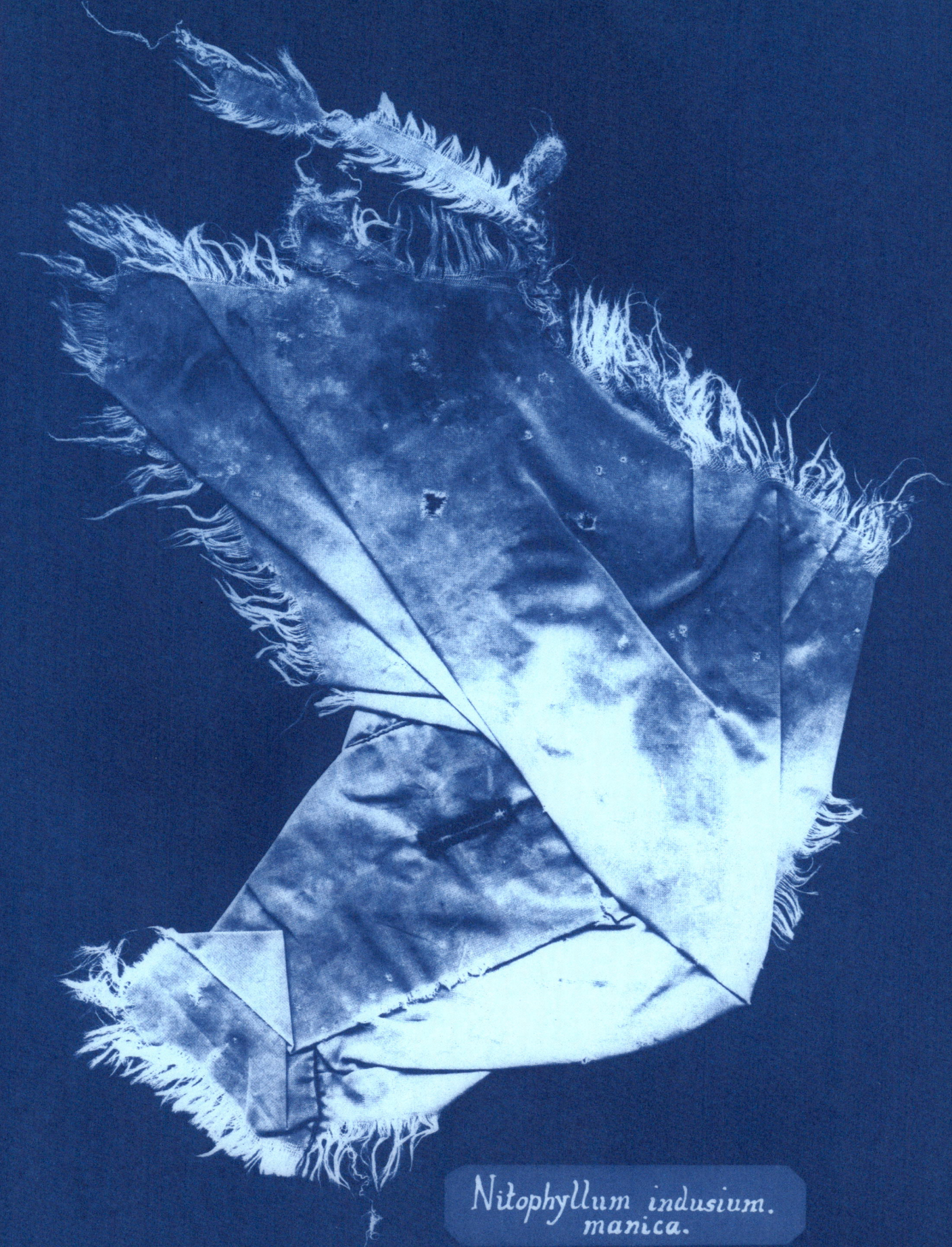

Nitophyllum indusium.
manica.

Shirt button hole

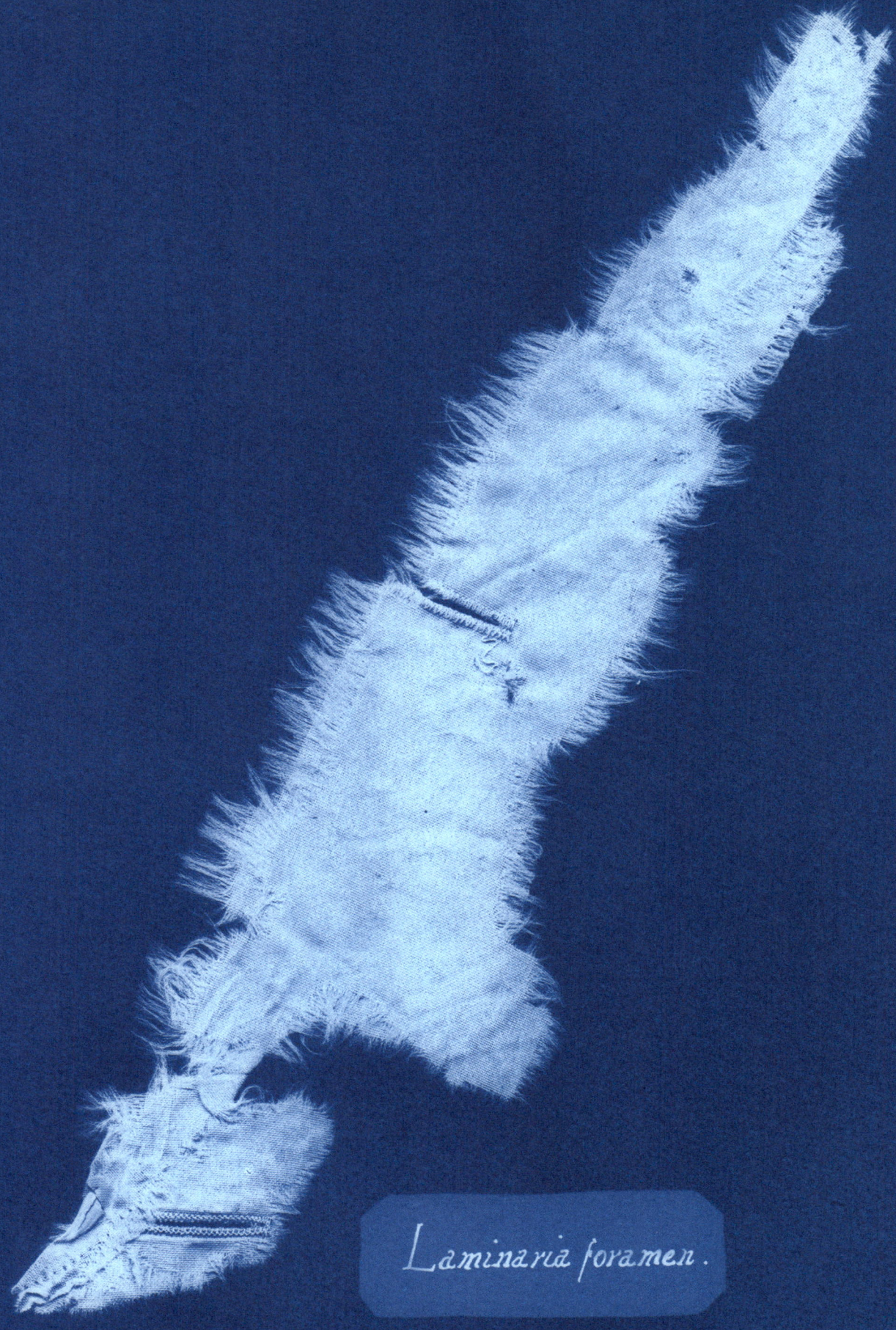

Laminaria foramen.

Top

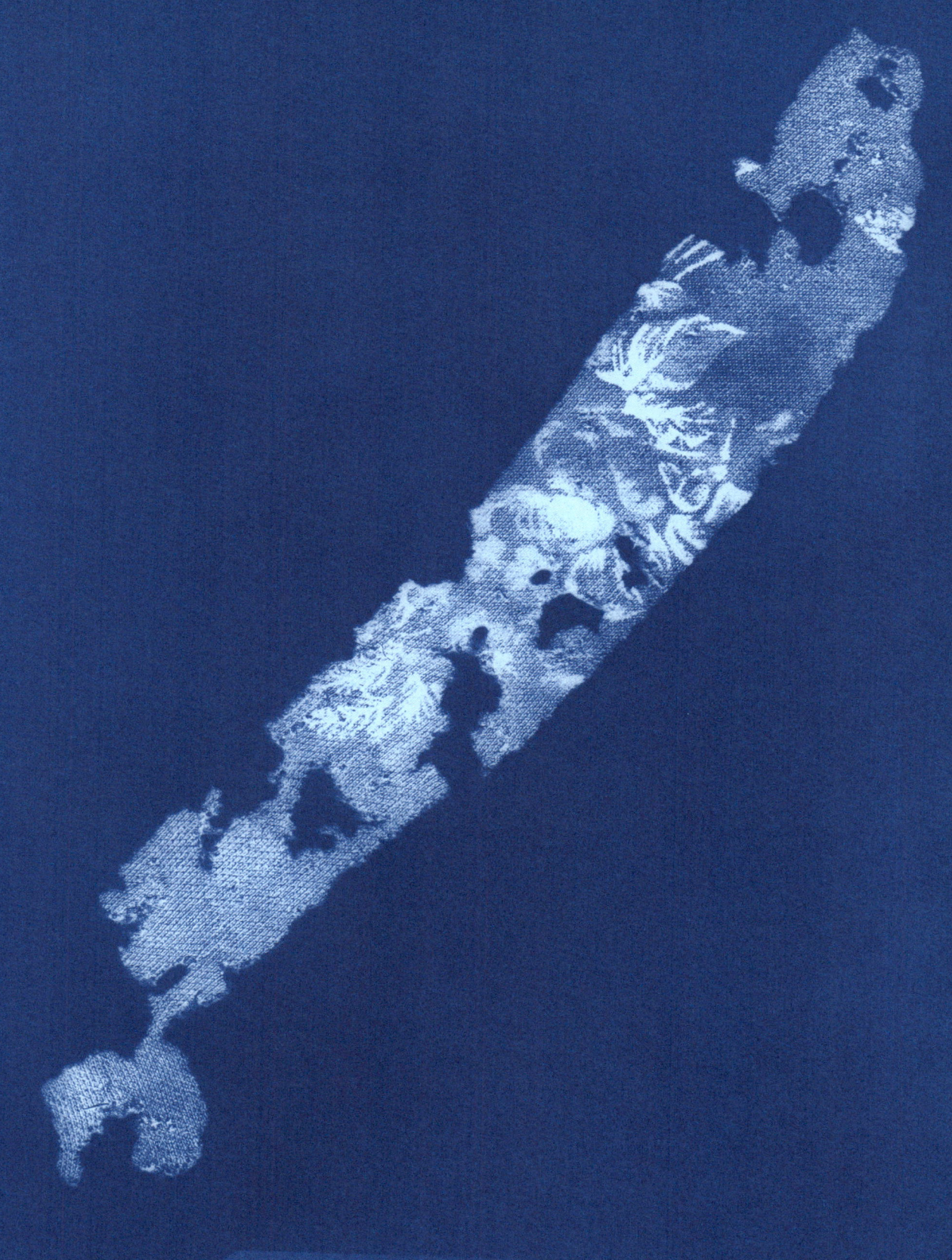

Laminaria folium.

Fine weave with thread

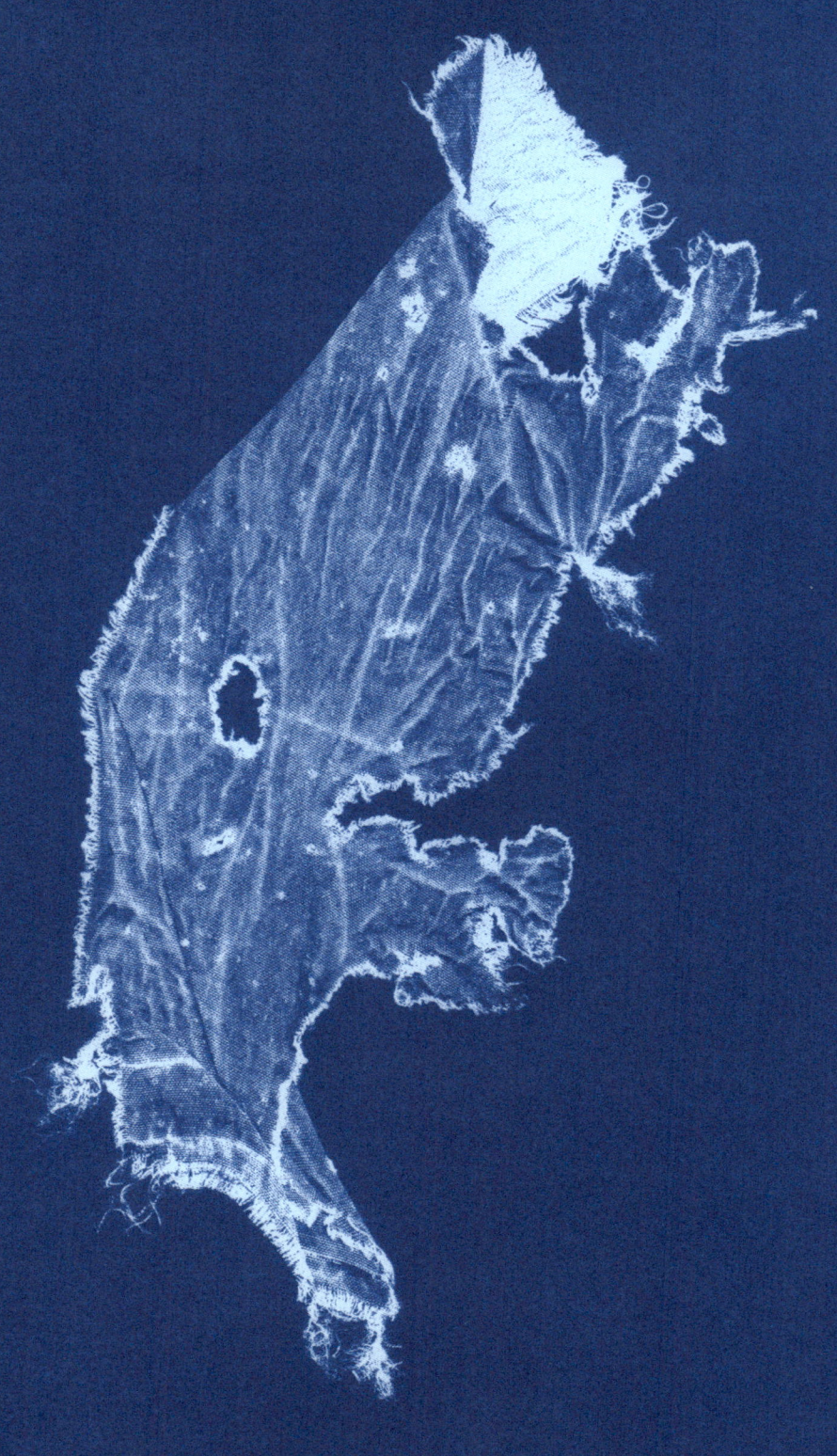

Rhodomenia imprimo

T-shirt

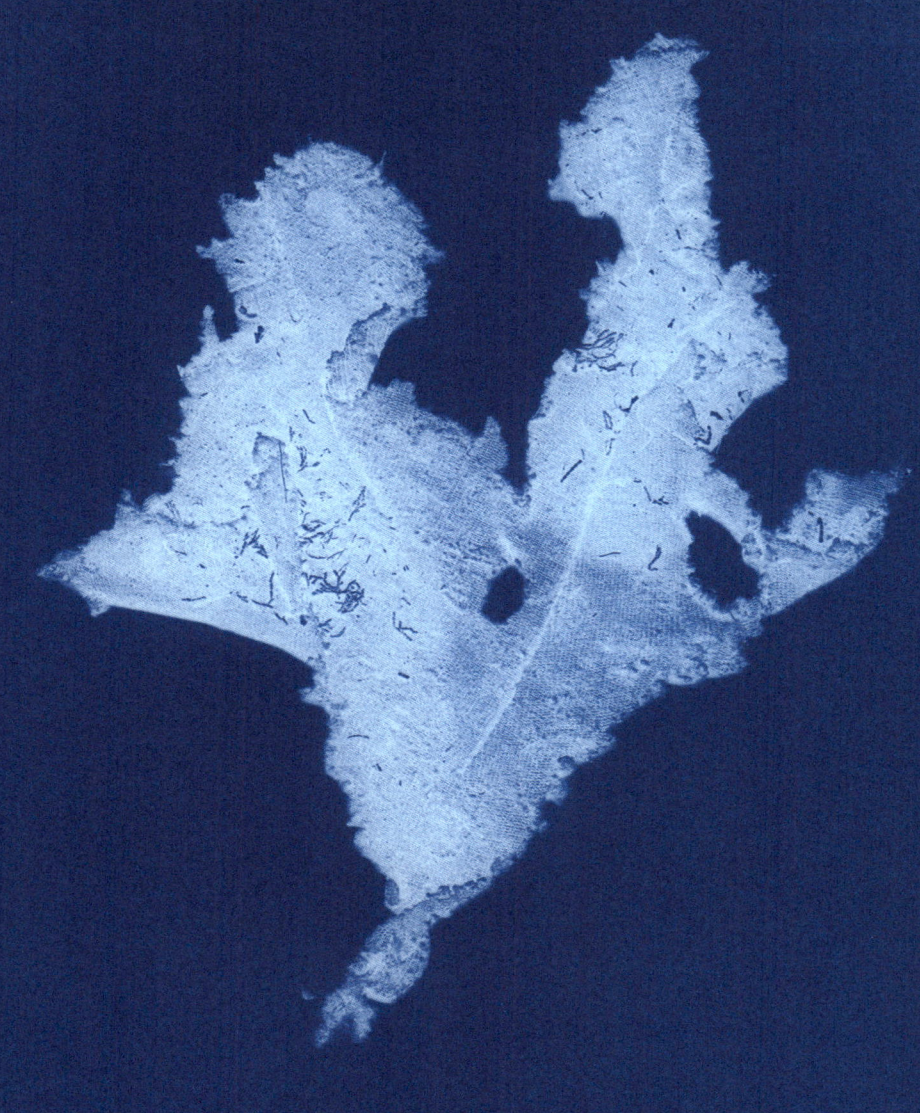

Padina sudor tunica..!

Striped T-shirt

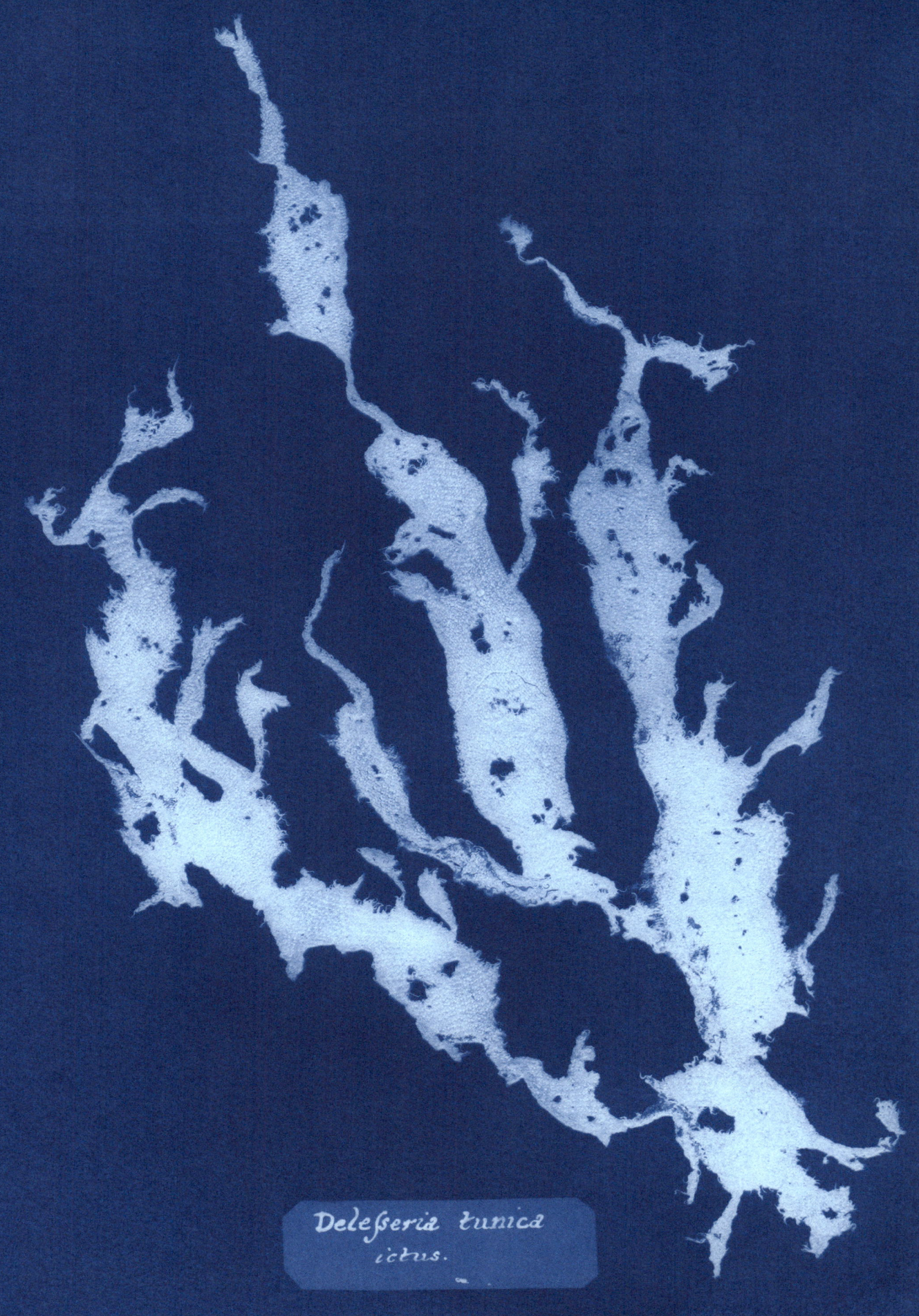

Delesseria tunica
ictus.

Mixed material

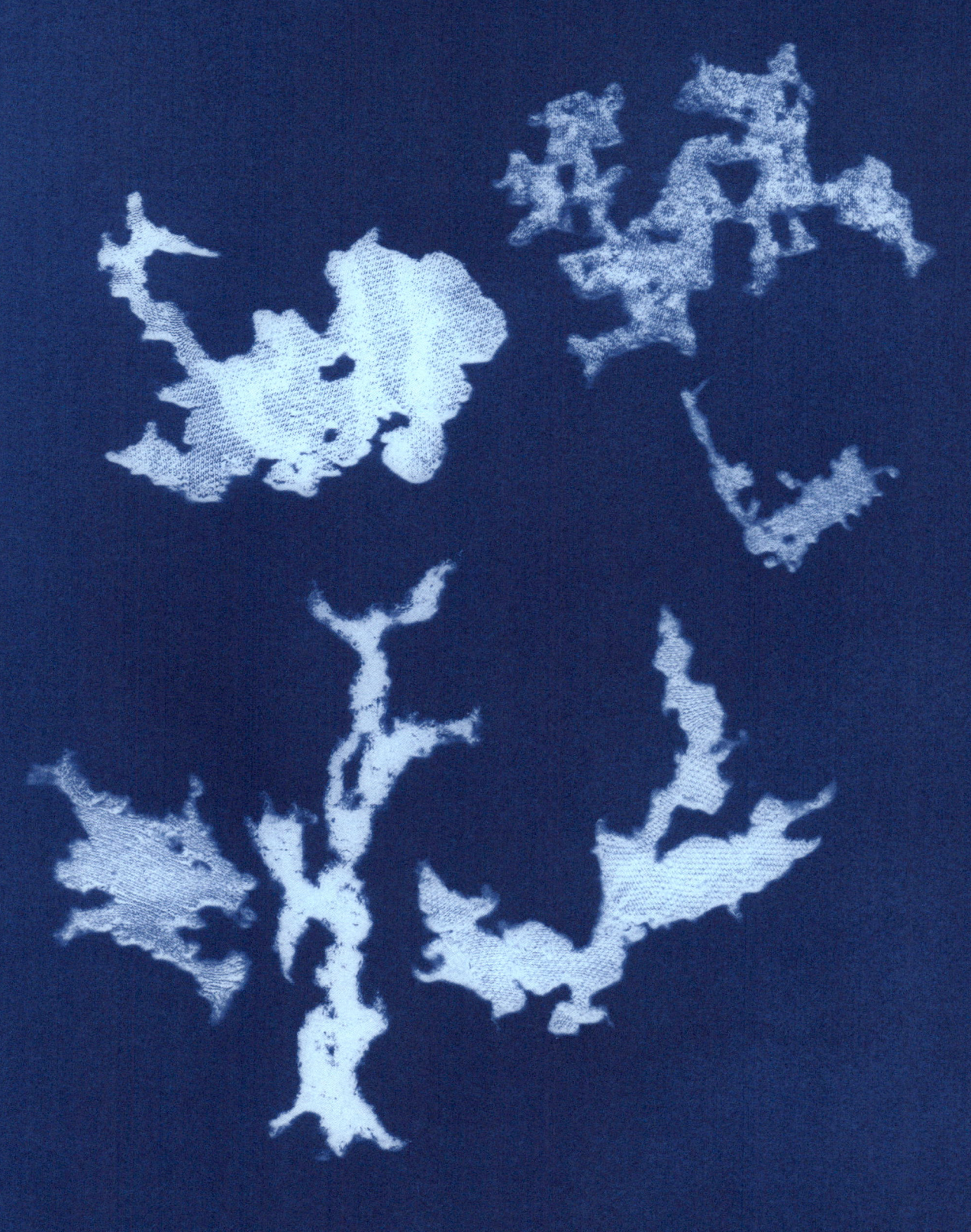

Rhodomenia mixtus.

School uniform skirt

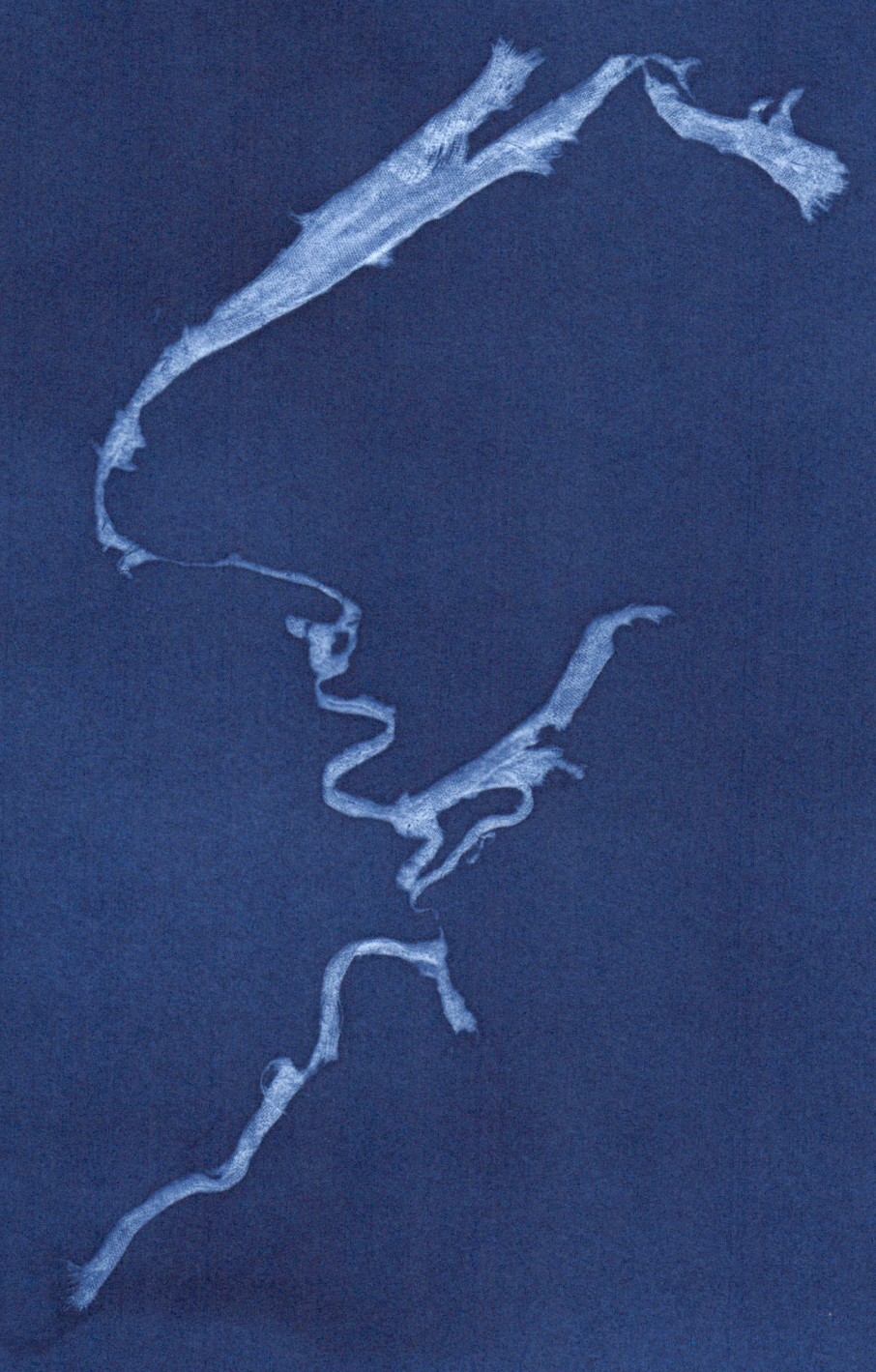

Enteromorpha vestis.
β navales.

Synthetic tartan kilt

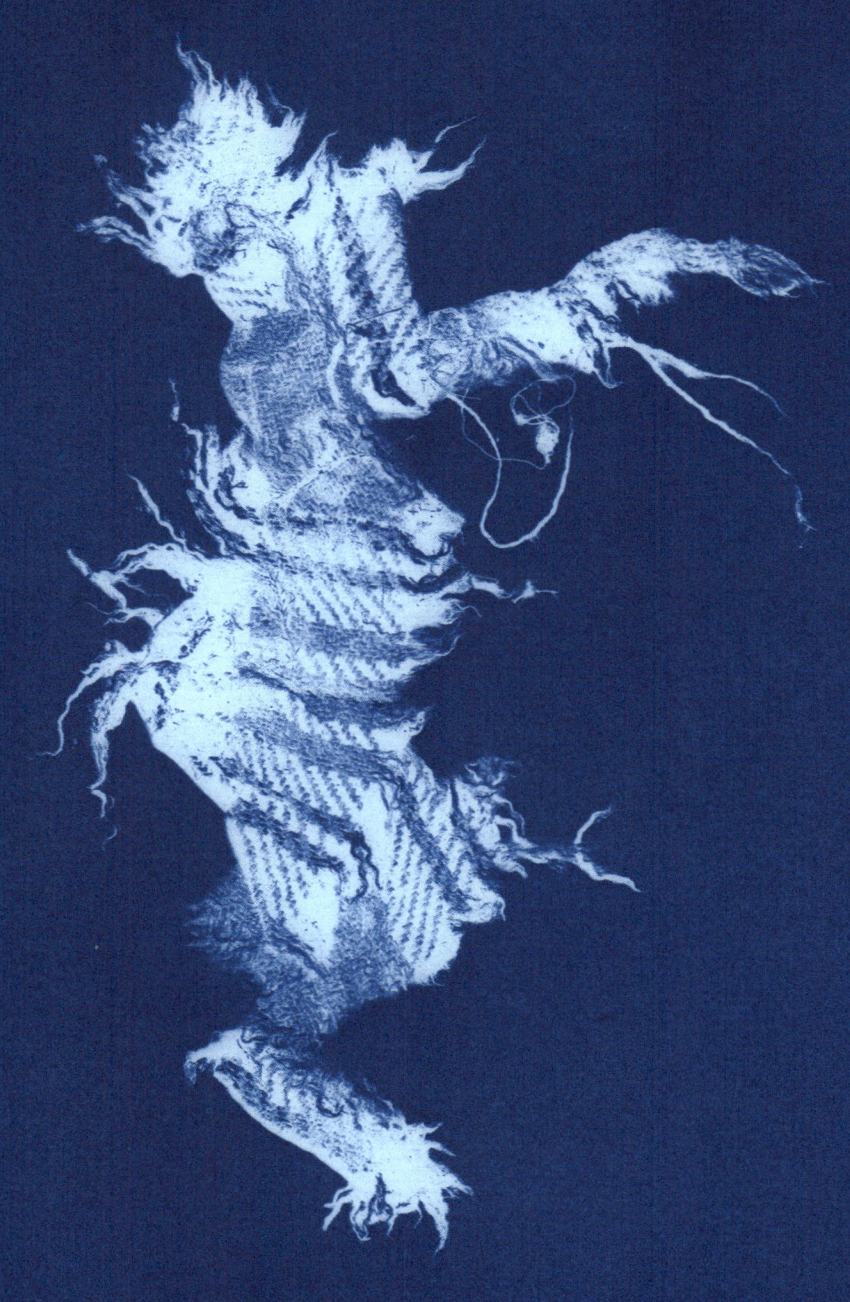

Rhodomenia materia

Synthetic fur hood

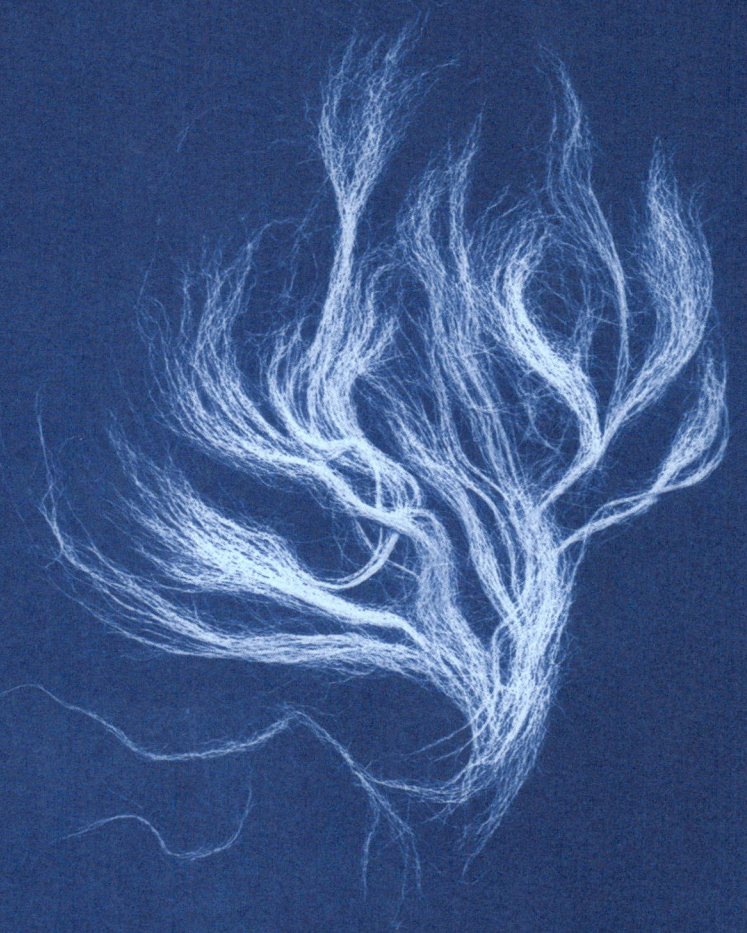

Myrionema palliolum.

Headscarf

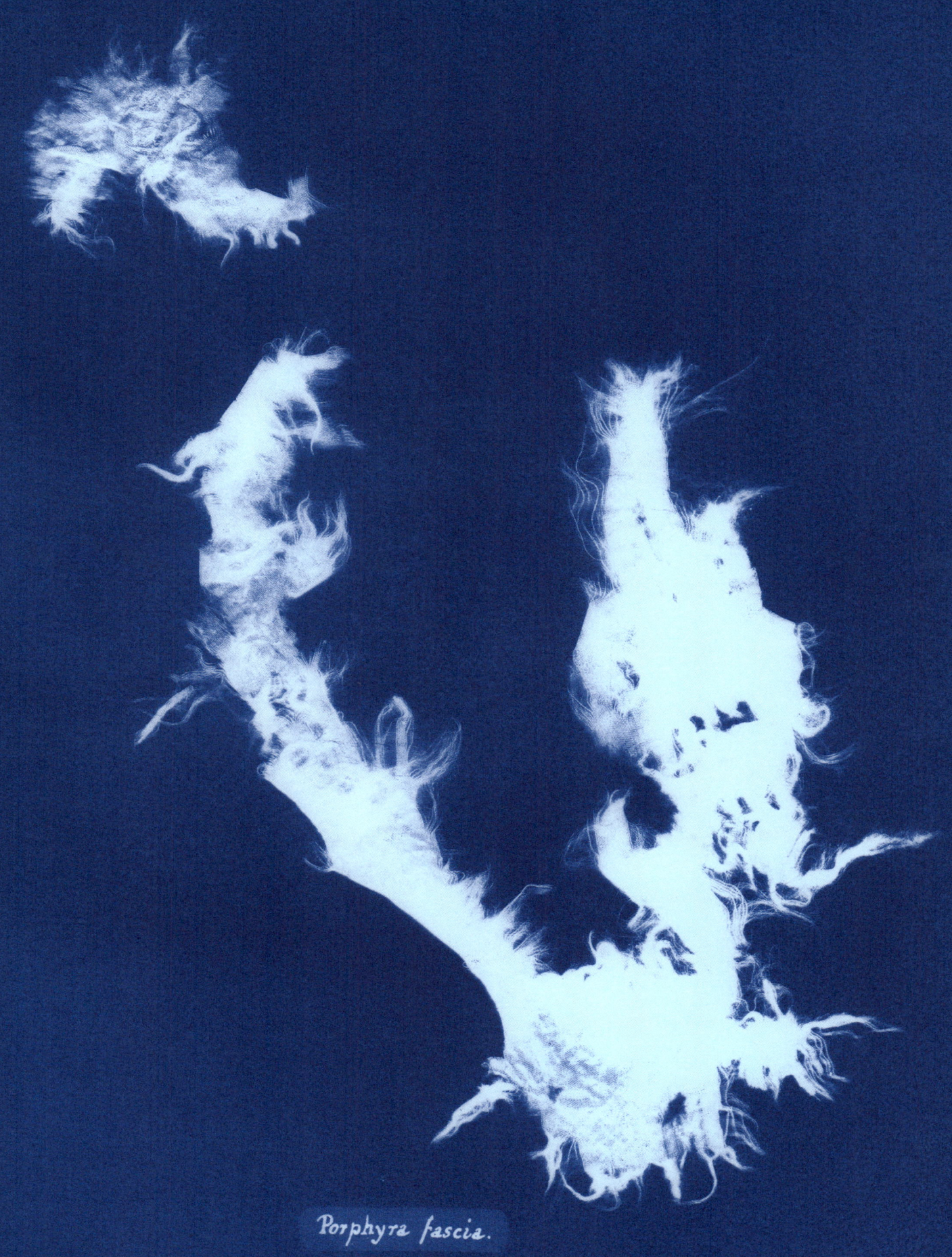

Porphyra fascia.

Cap

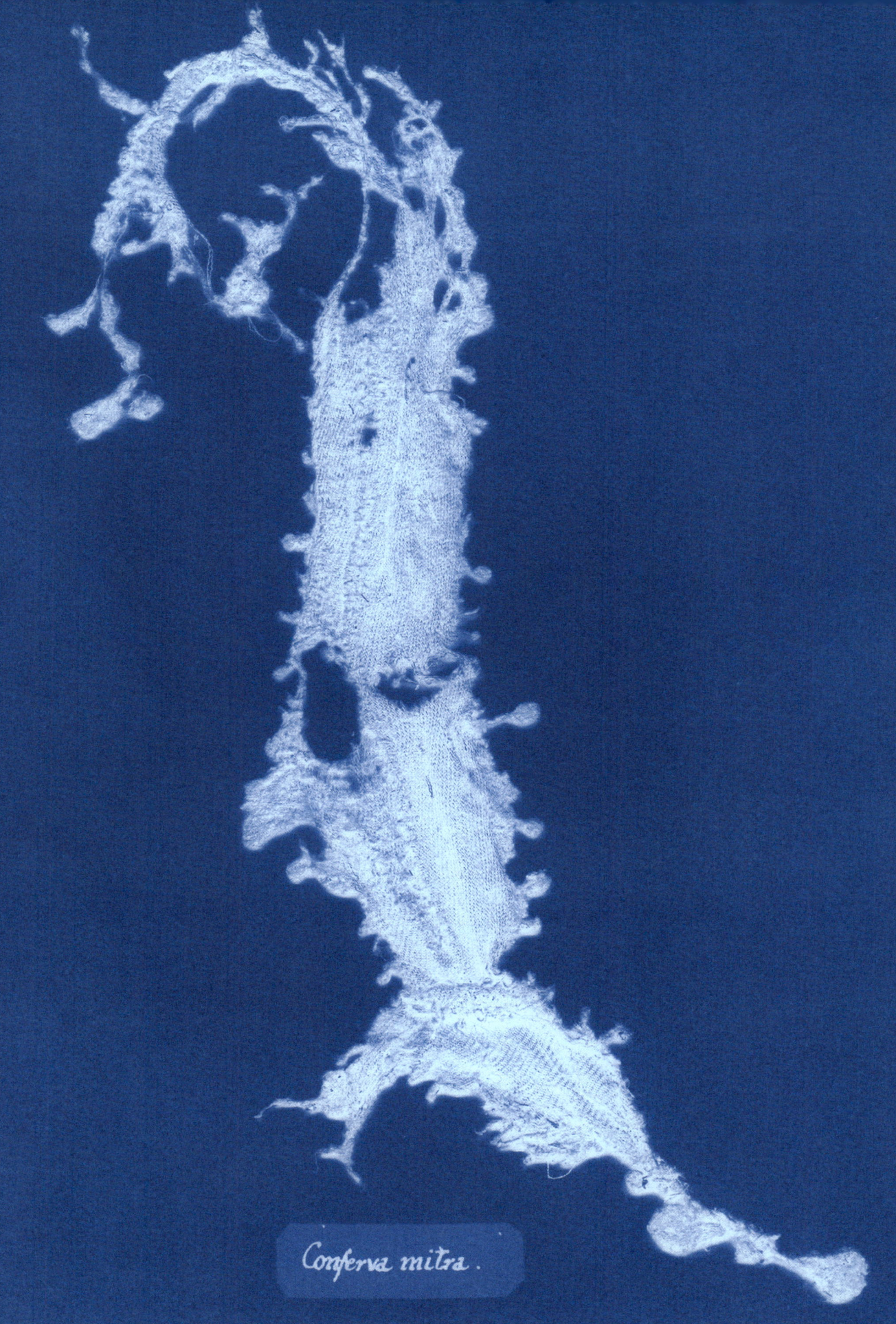

Conferva mitra.

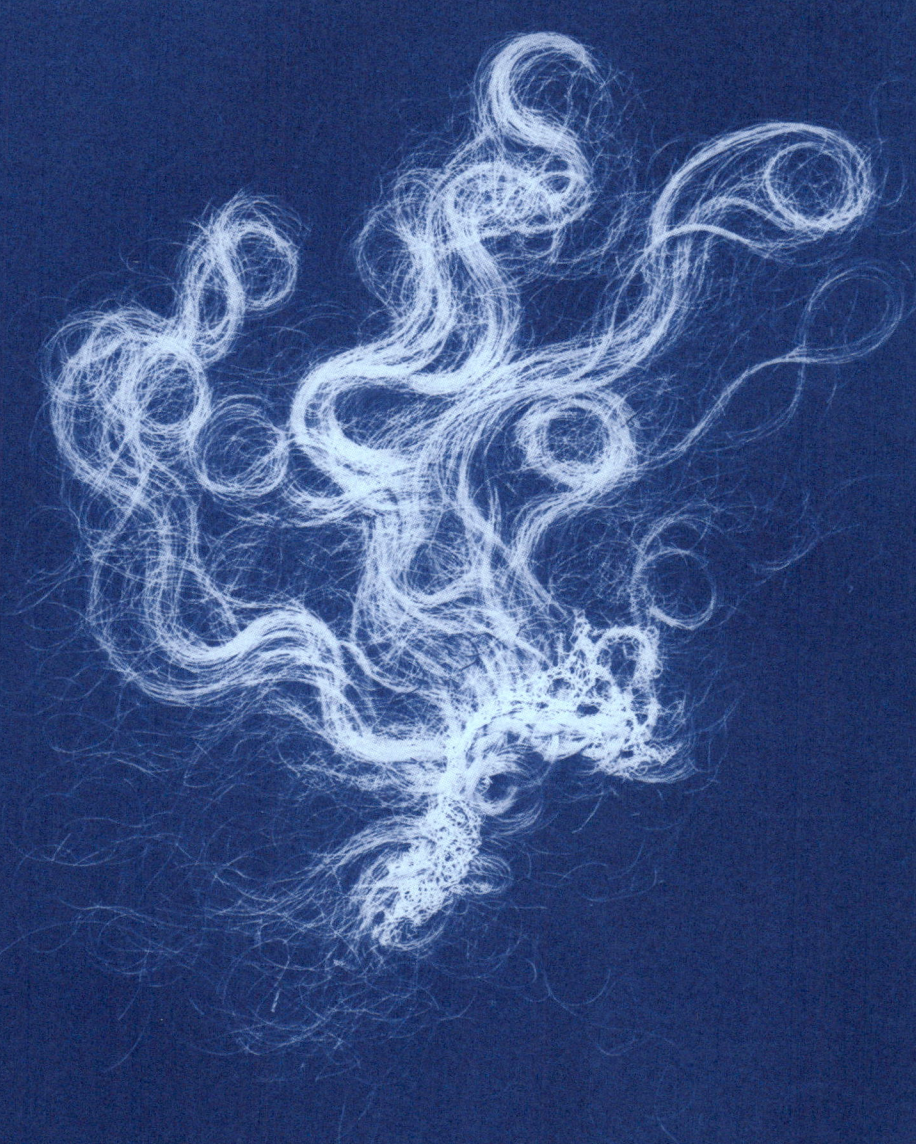

Fucus capillamentum

Ribbon

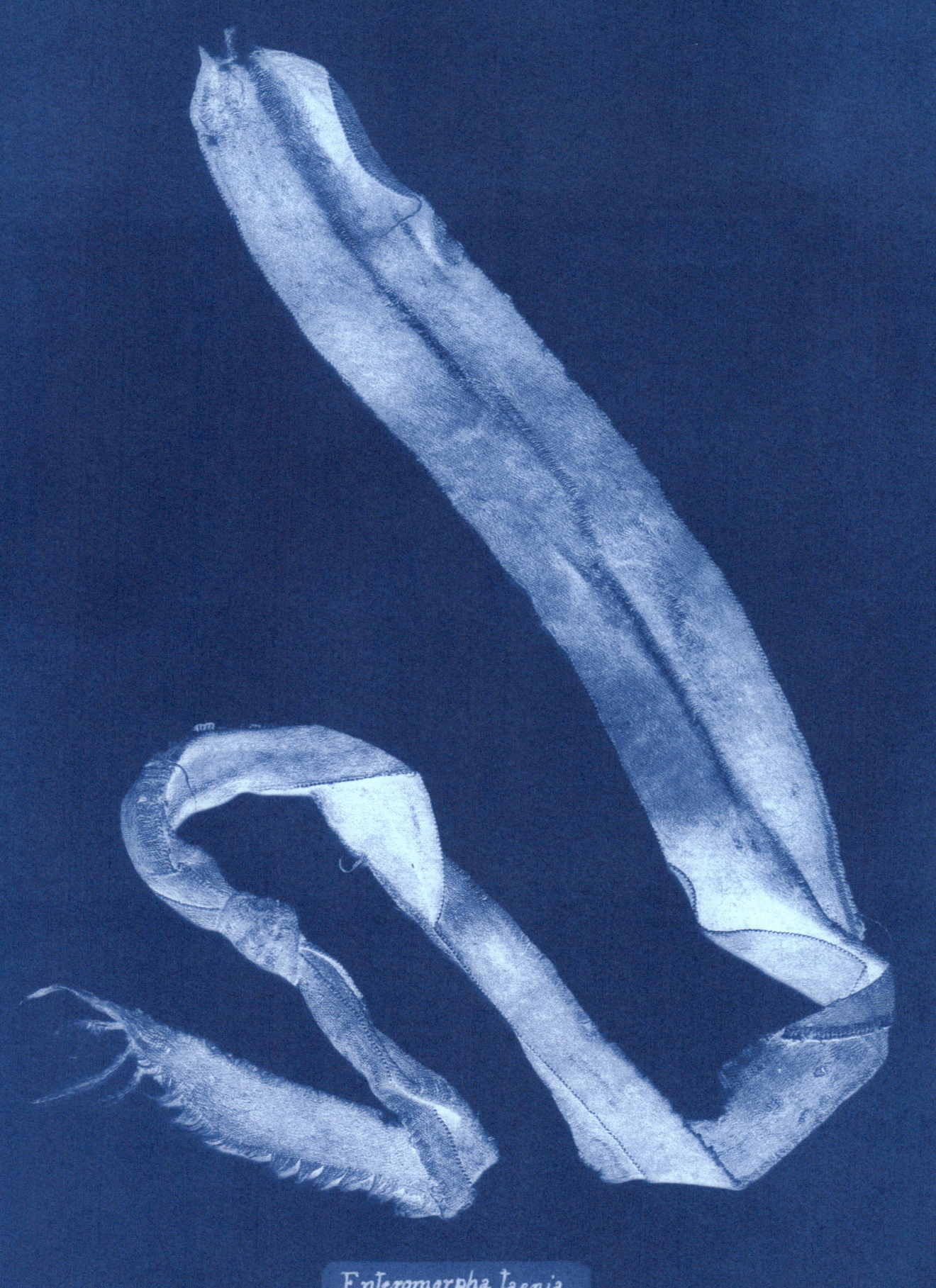

Enteromorpha taenia.

Dressing gown cord

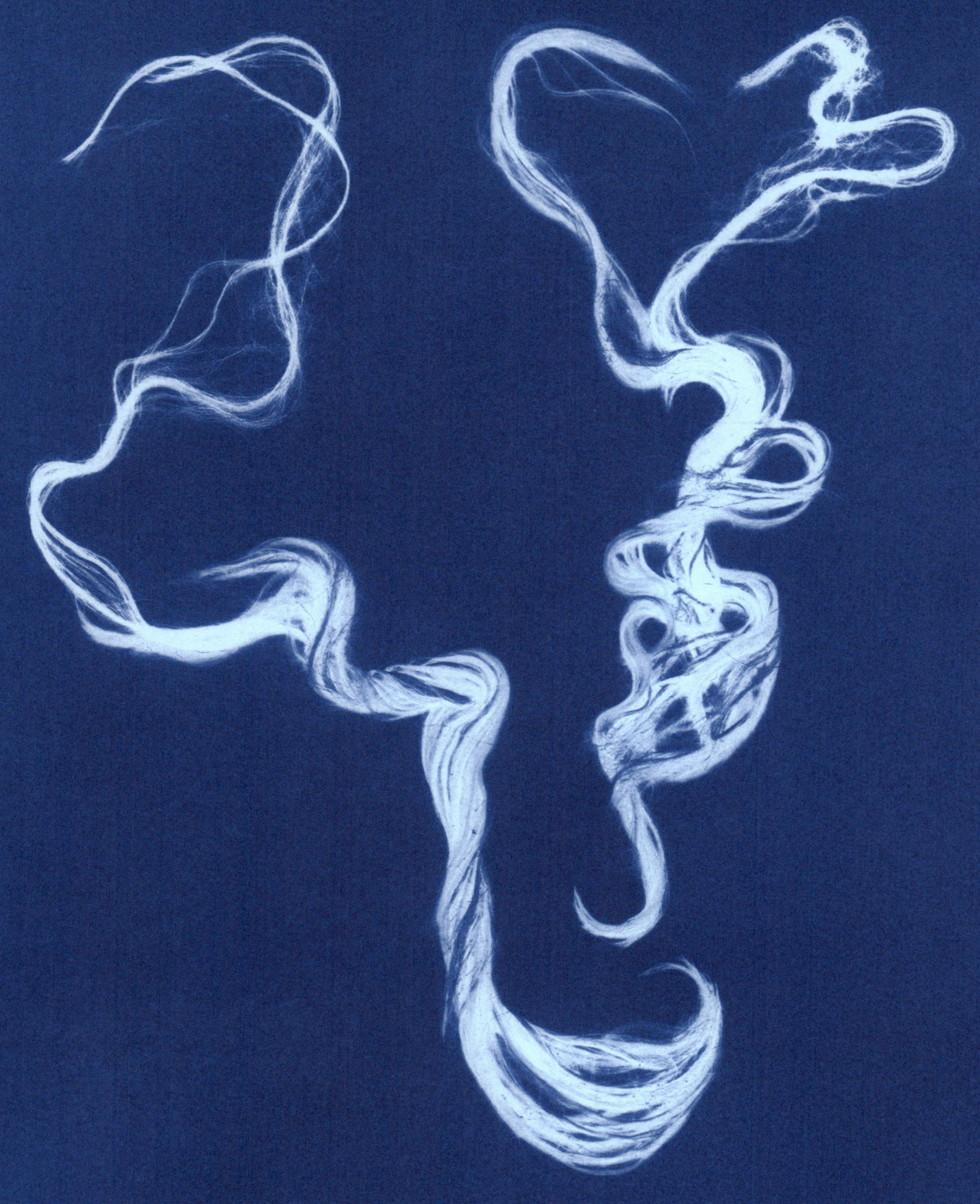

Conferva funis.

Pyjamas

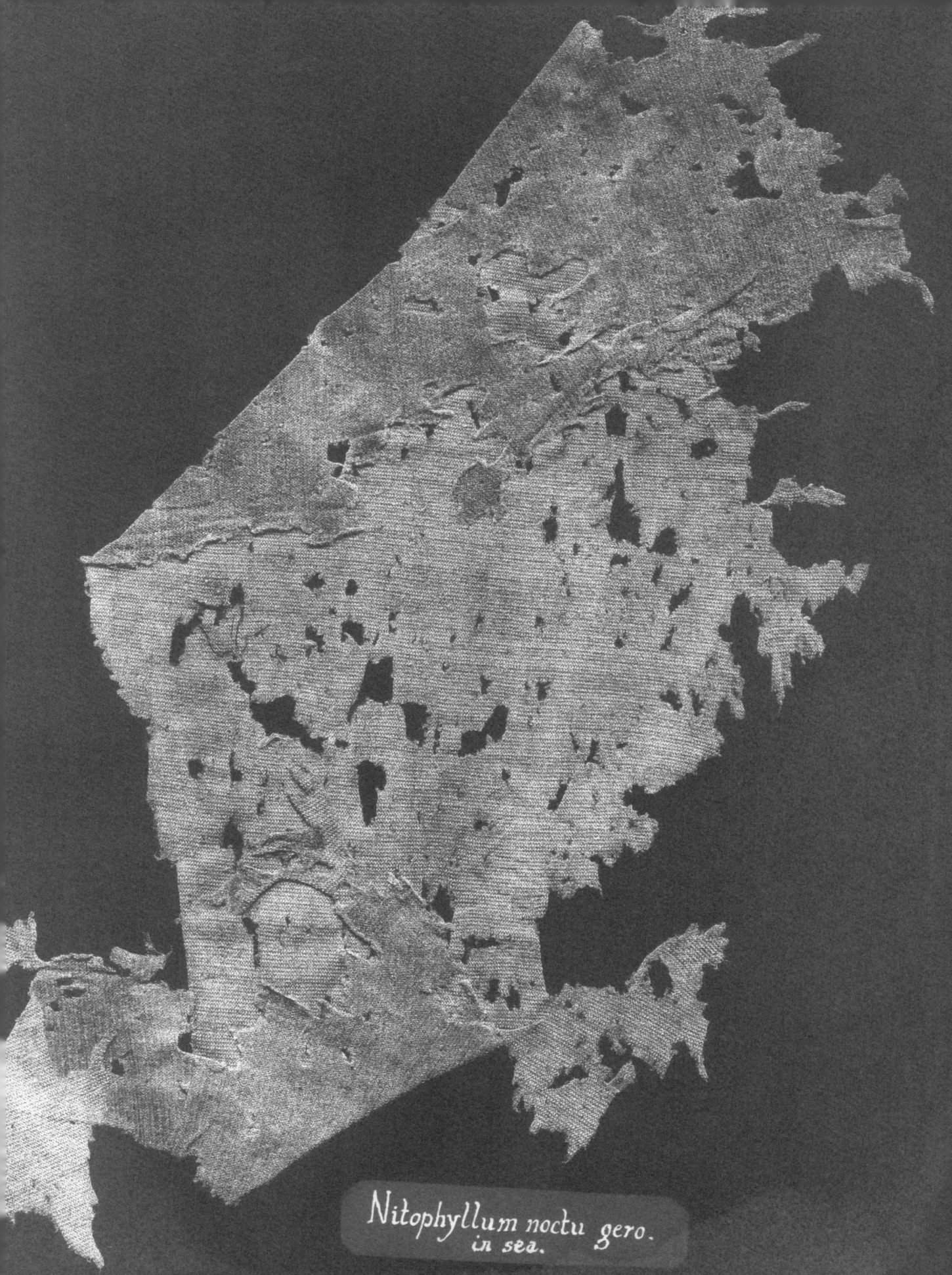

Nitophyllum noctu gero.
in sea.

Children's fancy dress

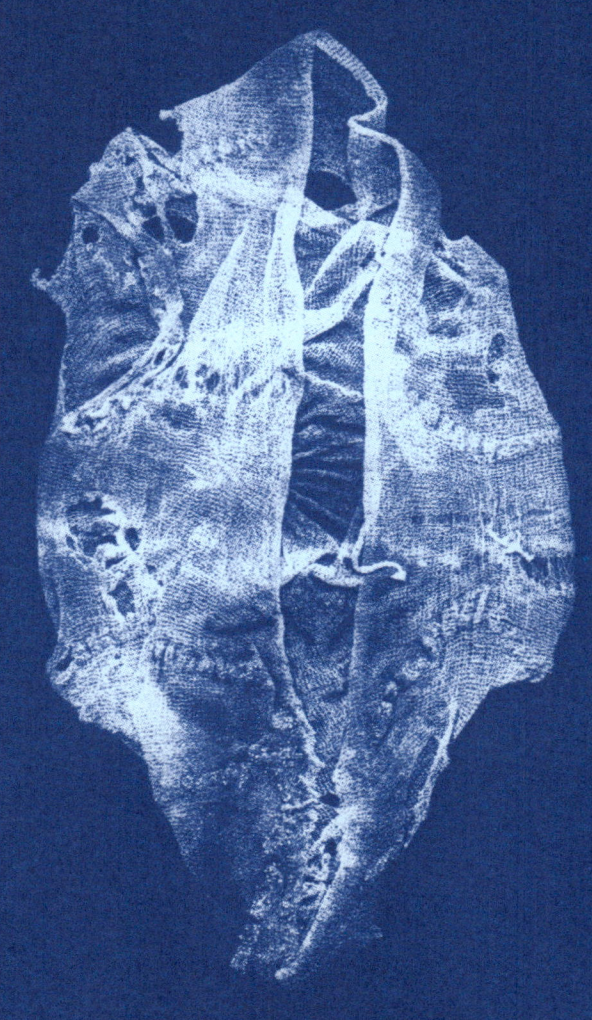

Rhodomenia pennae II.

Sweat band

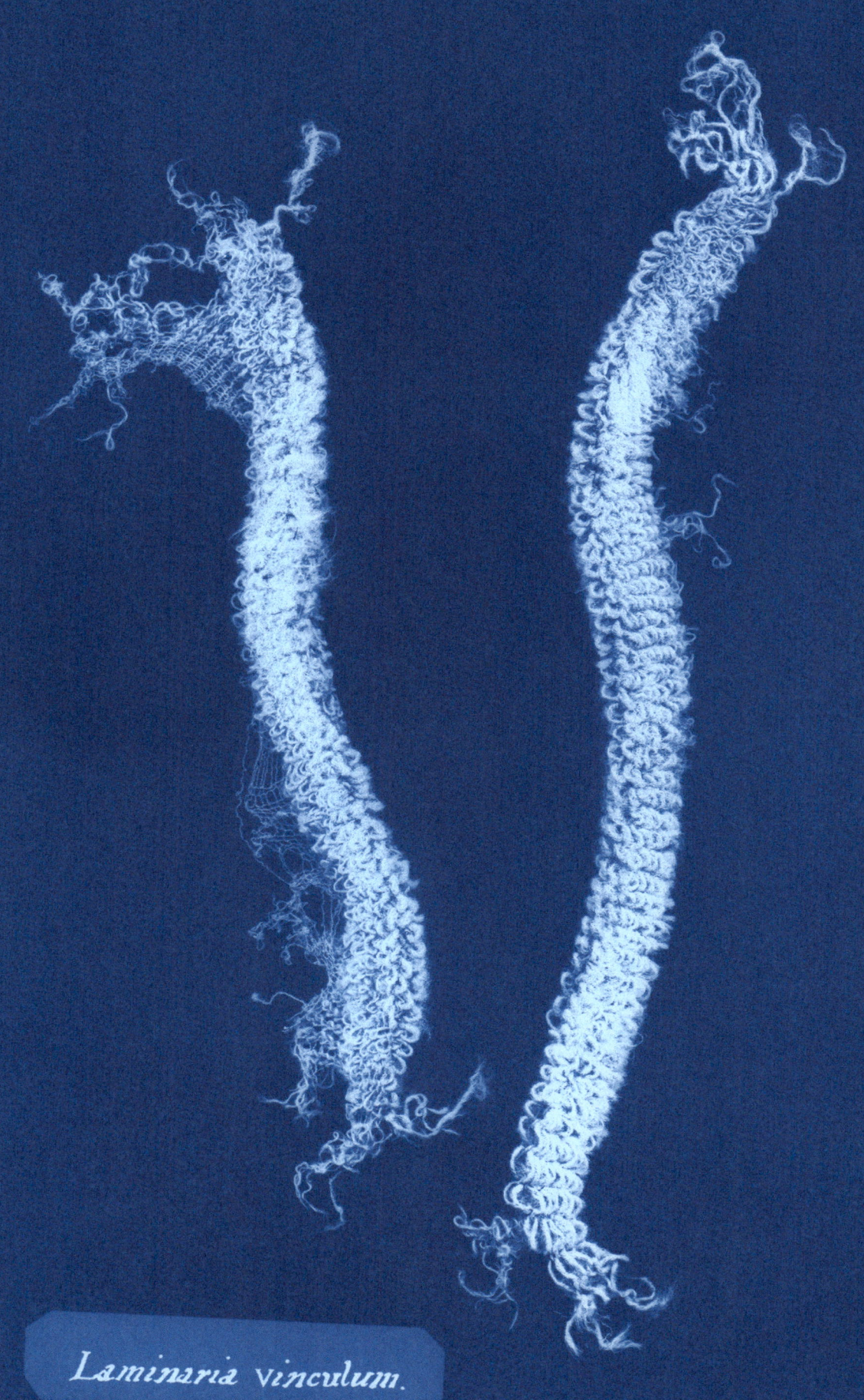

Laminaria vinculum.

Seam

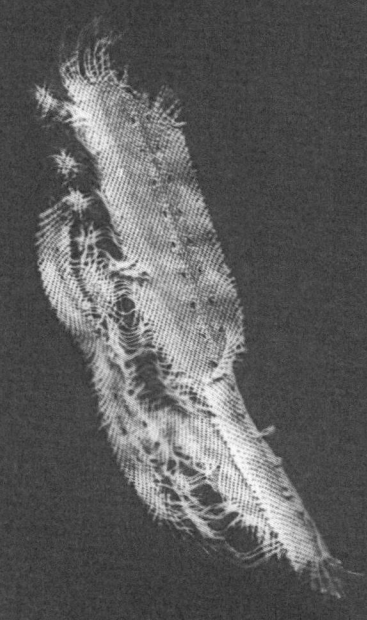

Calothrix sutura.

Netting

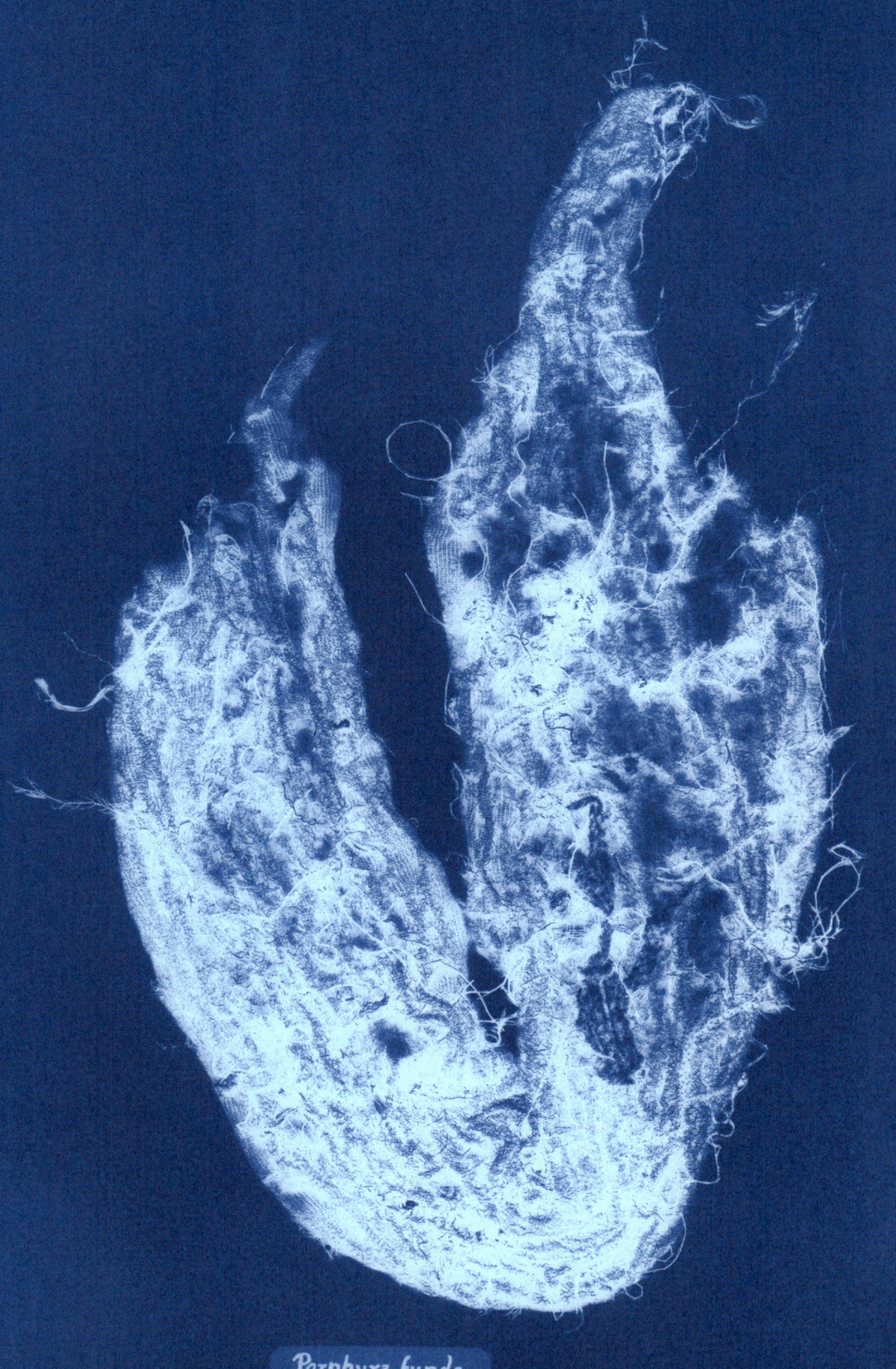

Porphyra funda.

Unknown materials

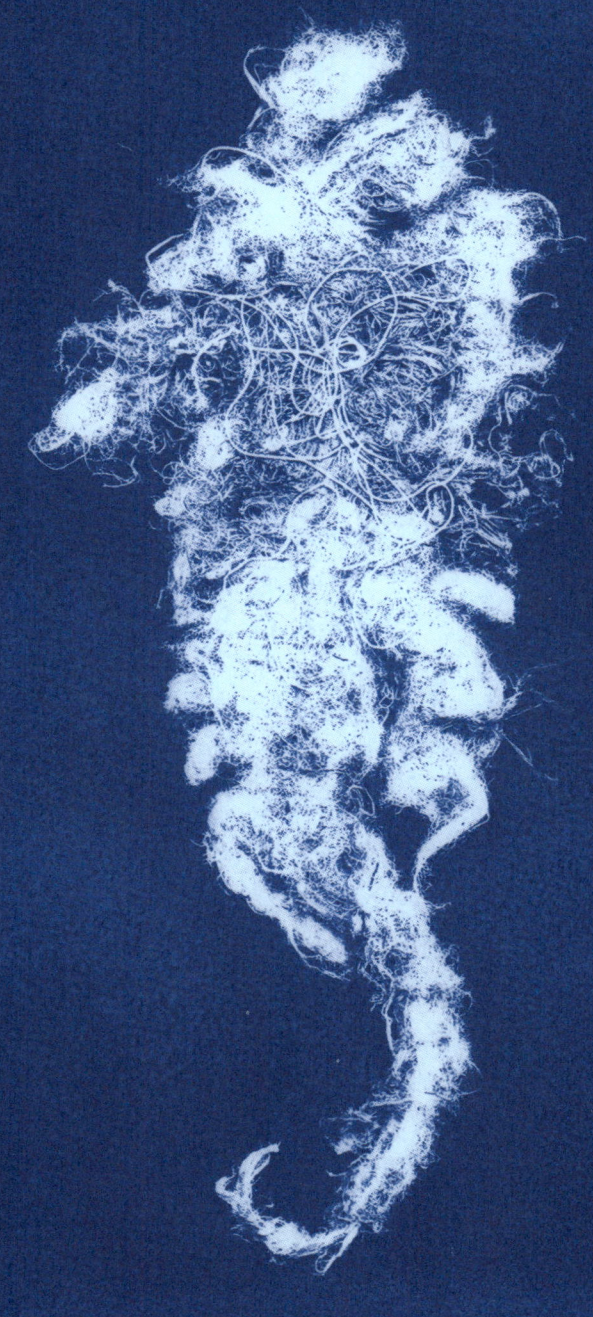

Ulva Concretus.

Velcro

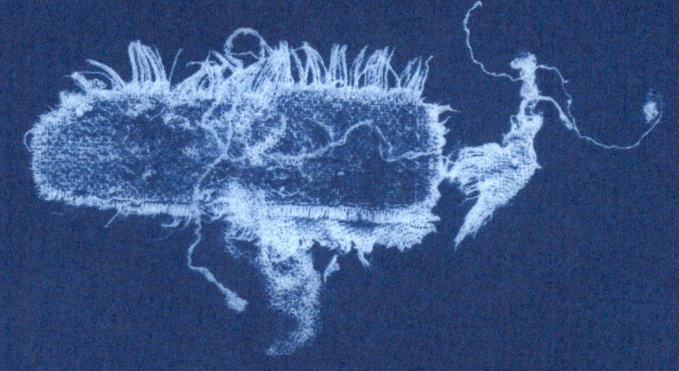

Conserva. inugo.

This Conserva, a few years ago
was recovered from the coastal
area of Yorkshire.

Elastine

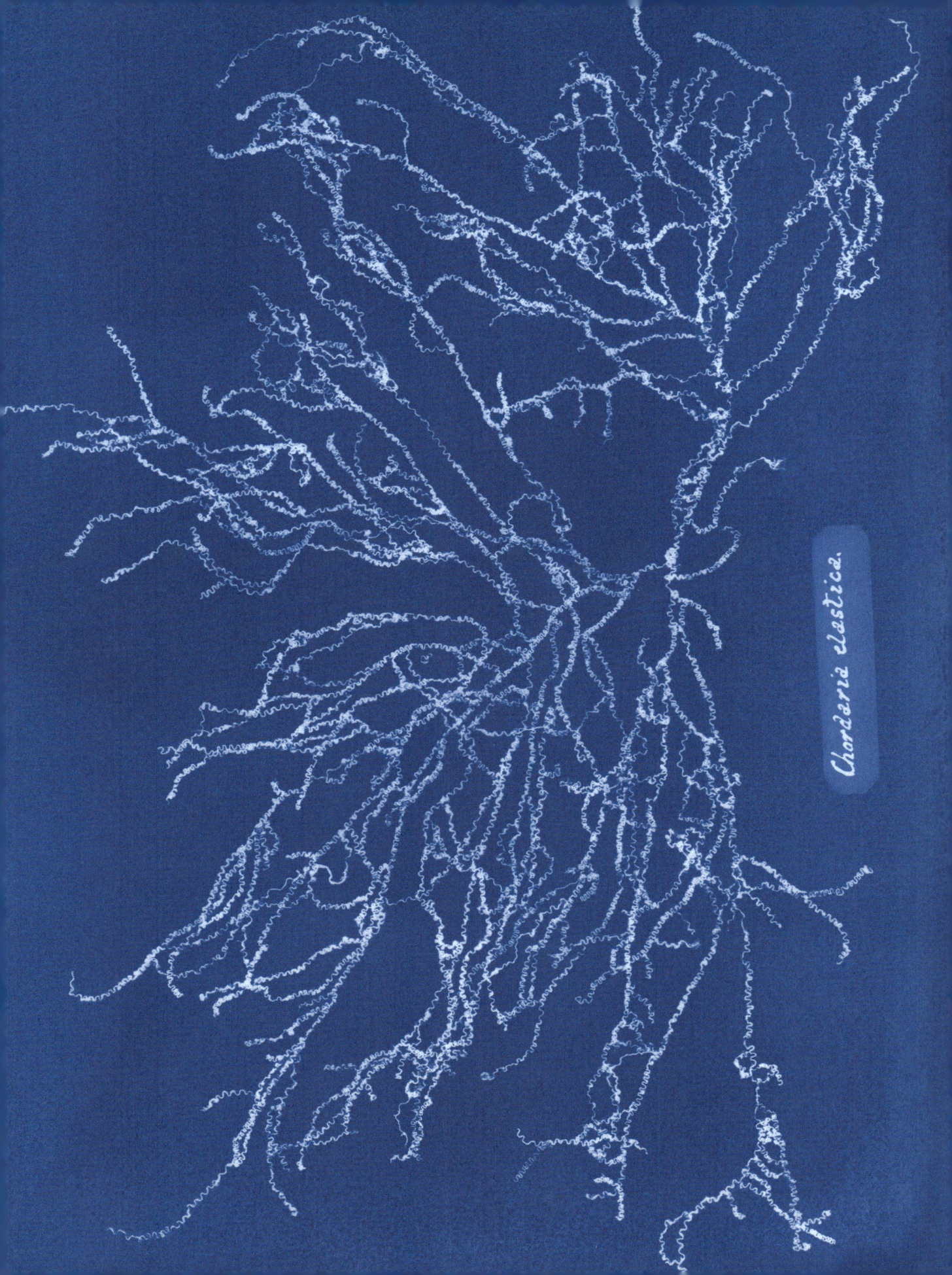

Chordaria elastica.

Lycra

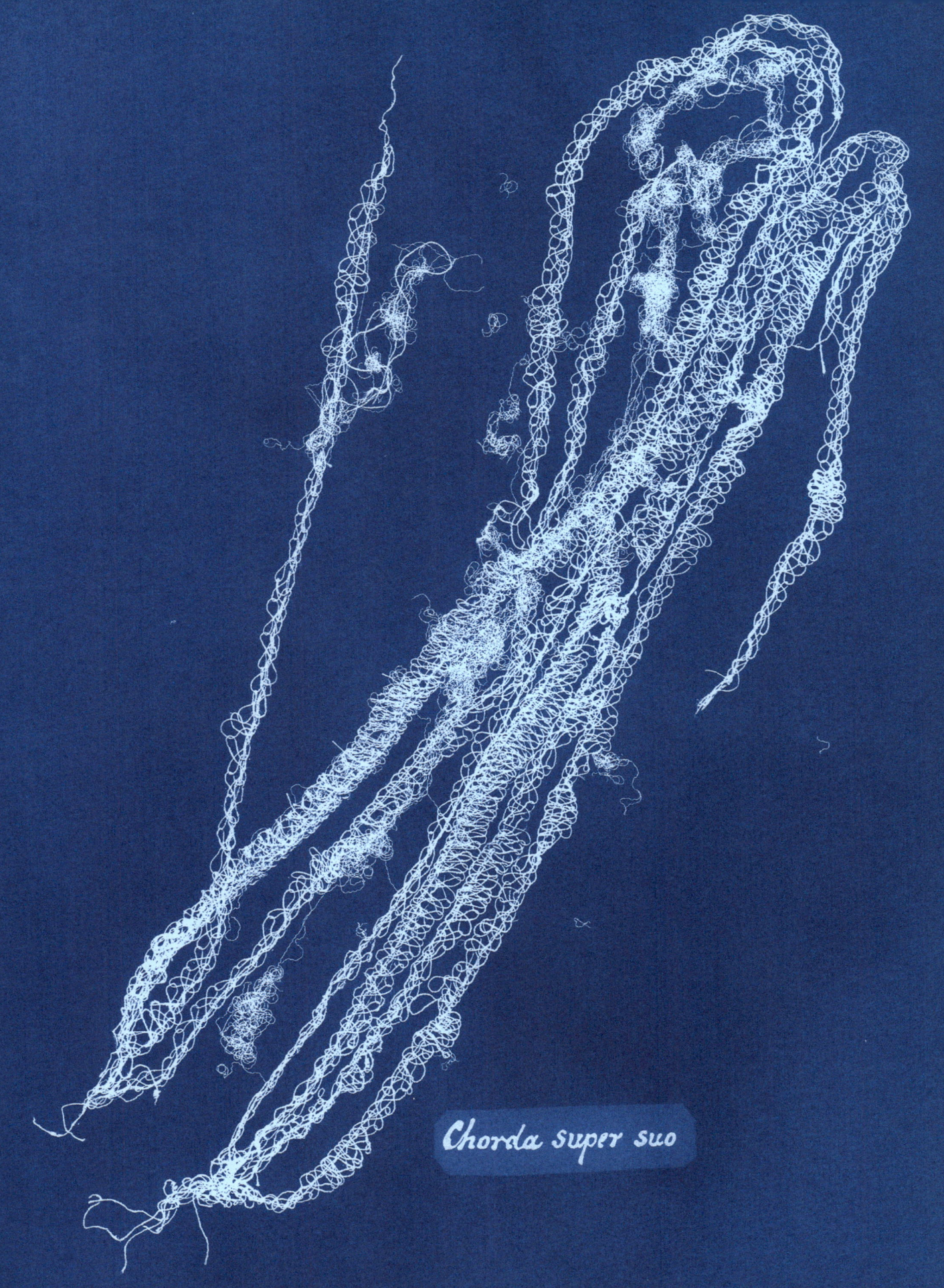

Chorda super suo

Hem

Laminaria limbus.

Zip

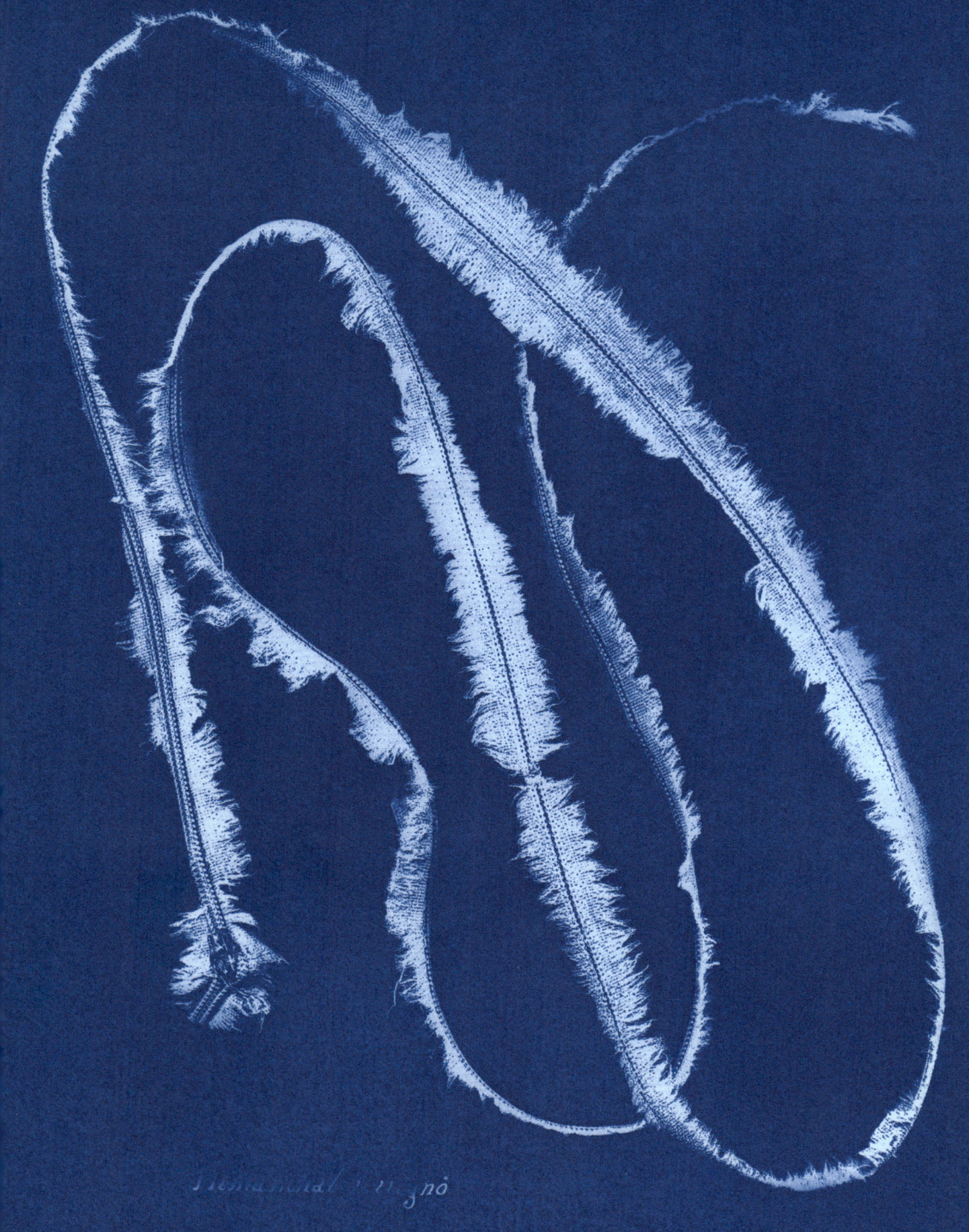

Pleat

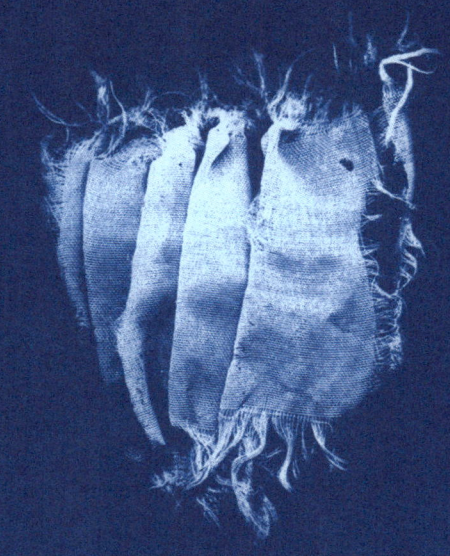

Callithamnion plico.

Shoulder pad

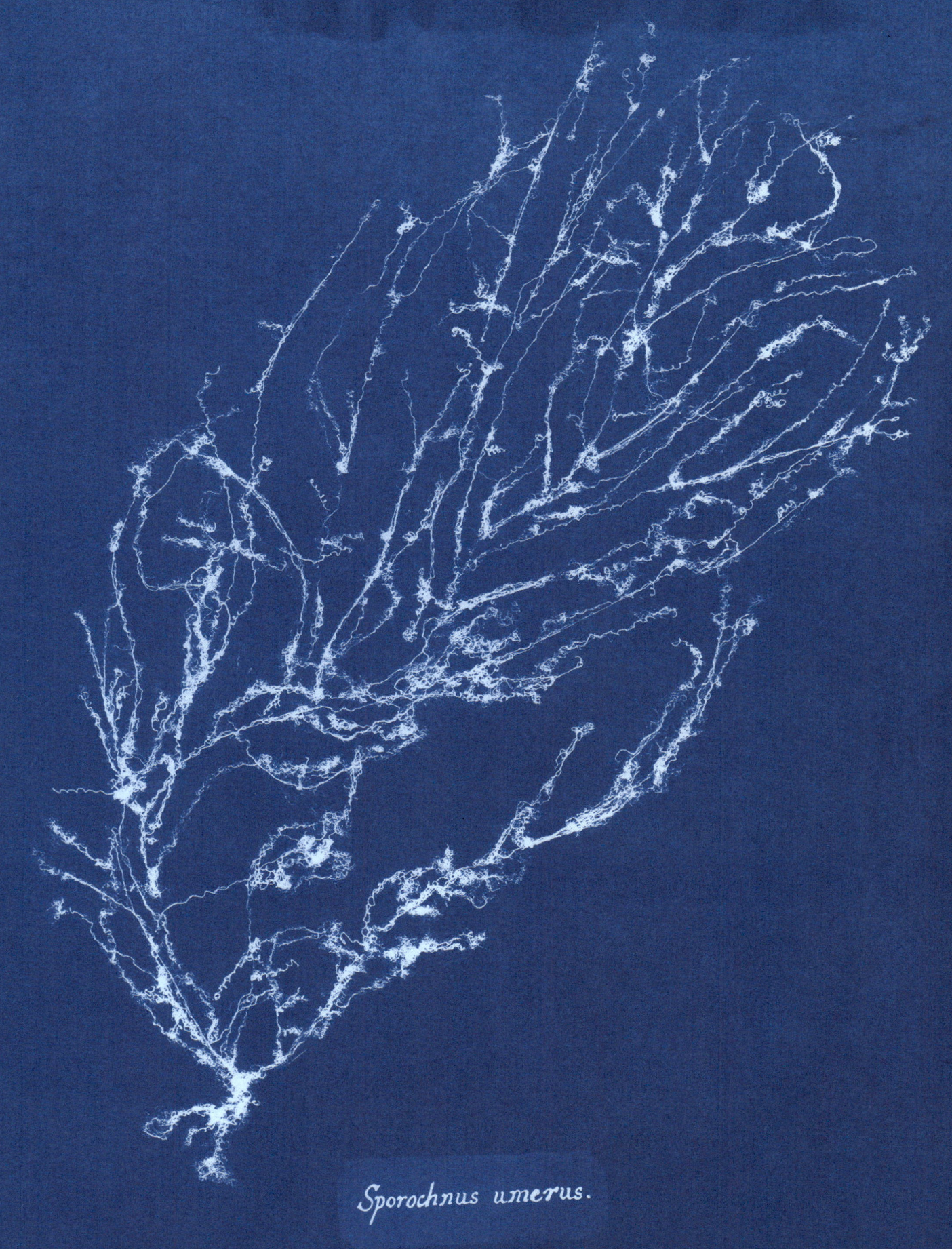

Sporochnus umerus.

Knitted collar

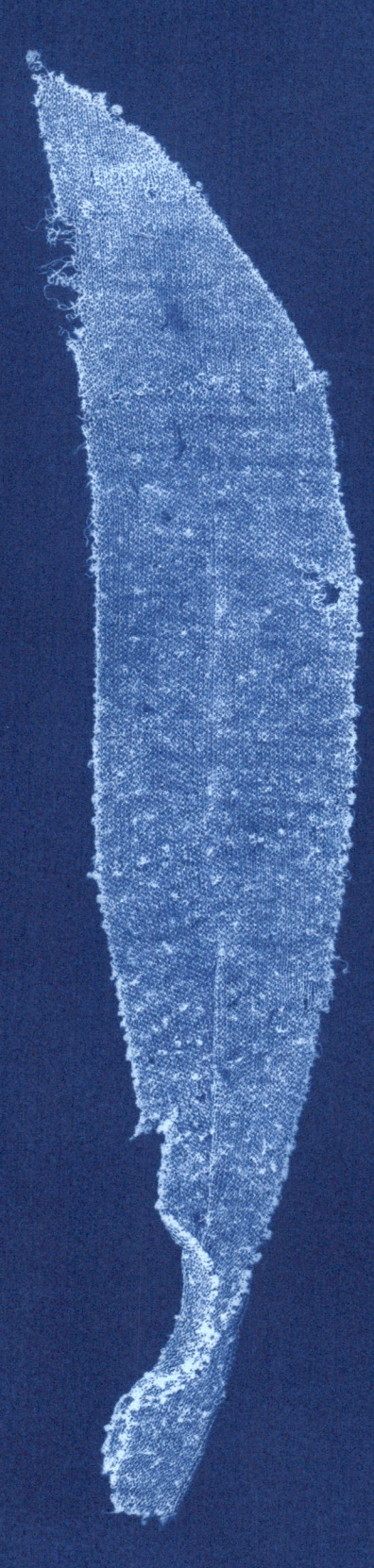

Punctaria collare.

Rouched strip

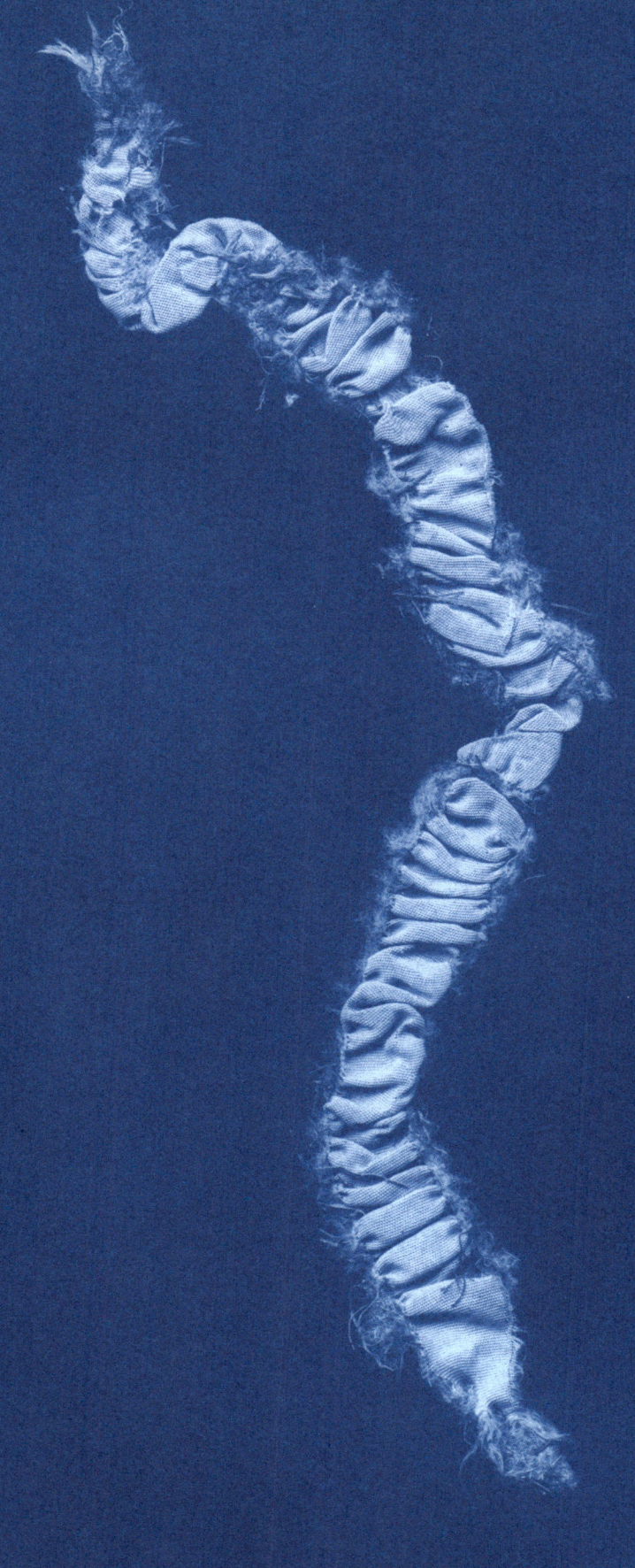

Fine weave

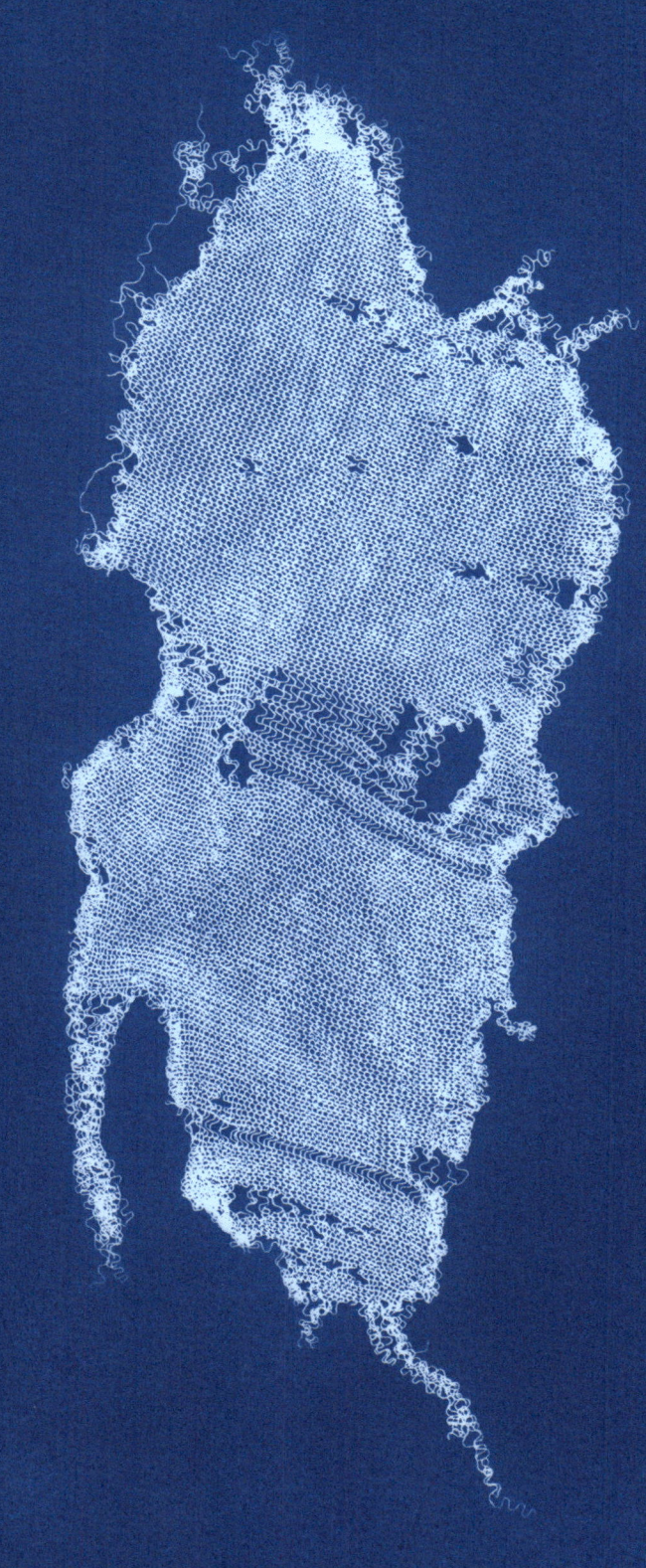

Punctaria scalae arum.

Threads

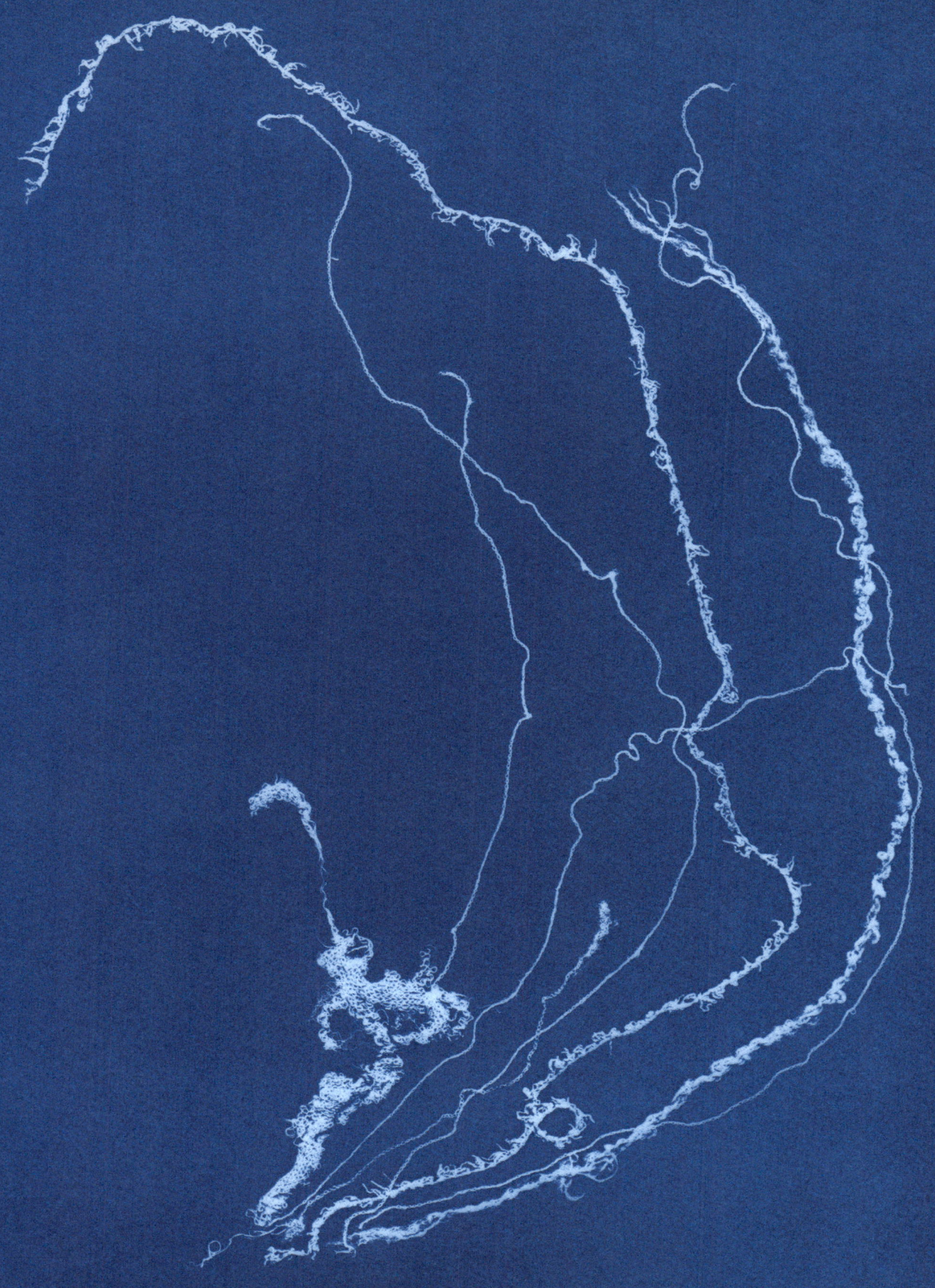

Chorda separatum.

Mixed fibres

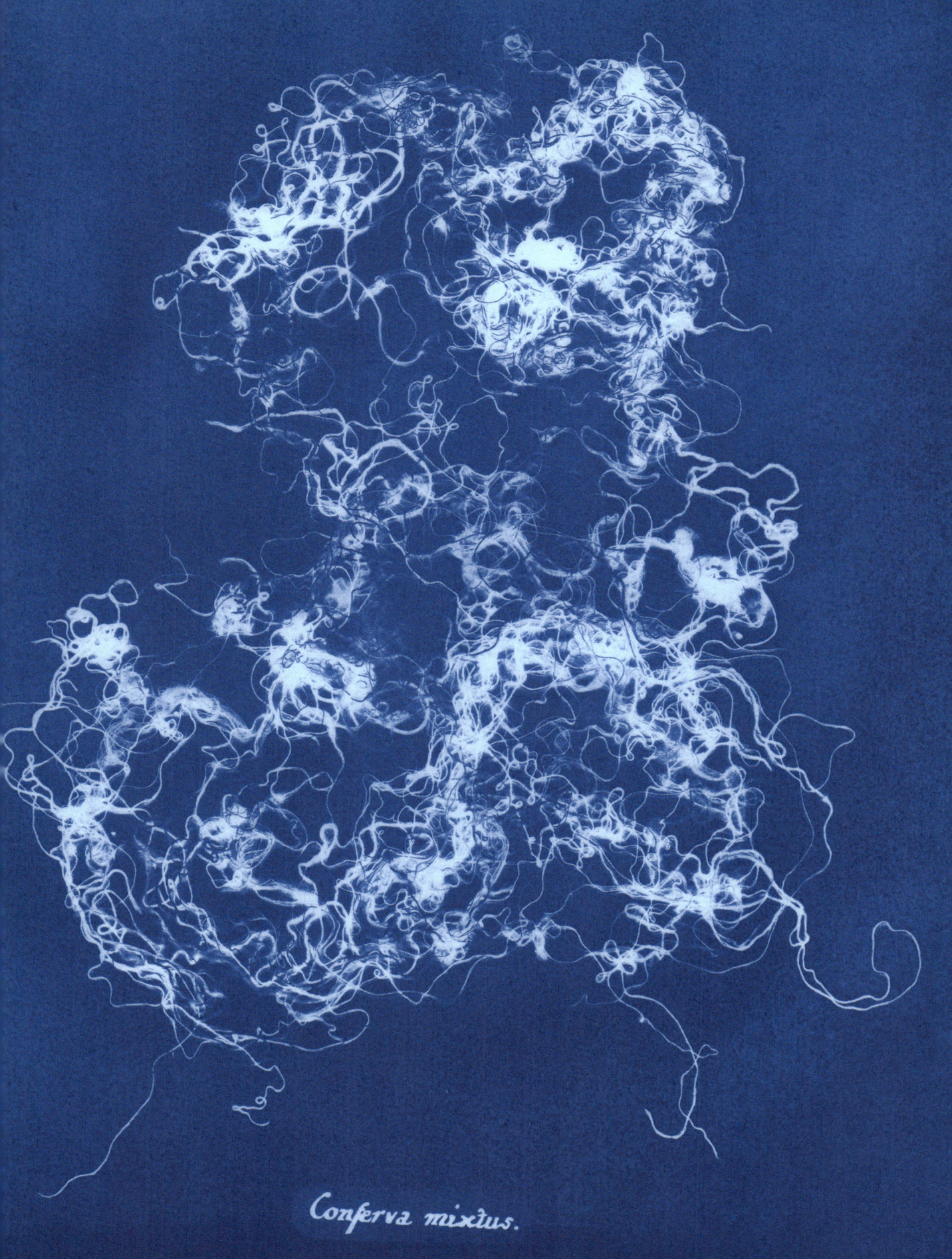

Conferva mixtus.

Mixed fibres with acrylic

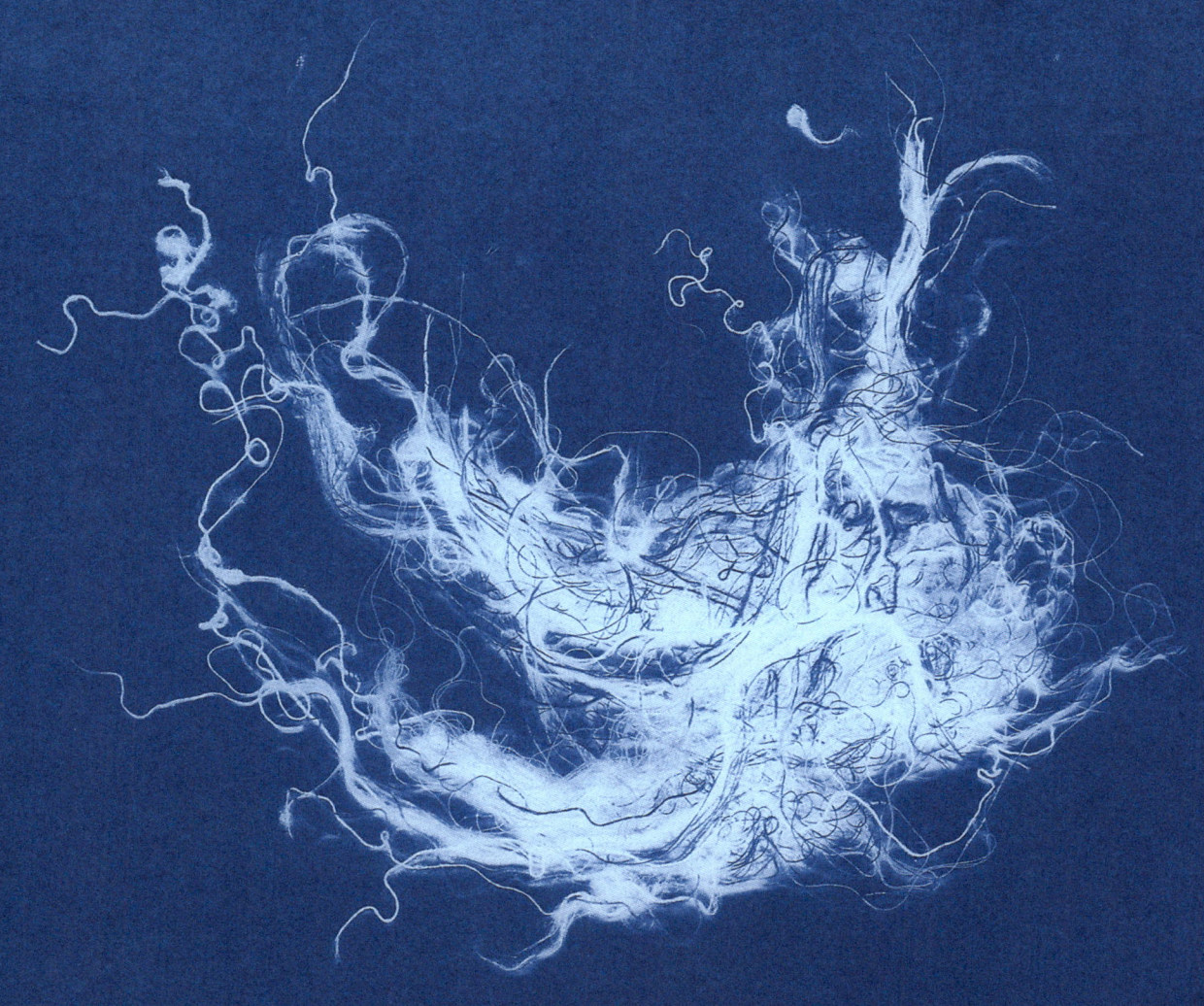

Conferva tibia.

Microfibres

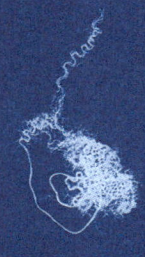

Conferva filum. II.

Synthetic mesh label

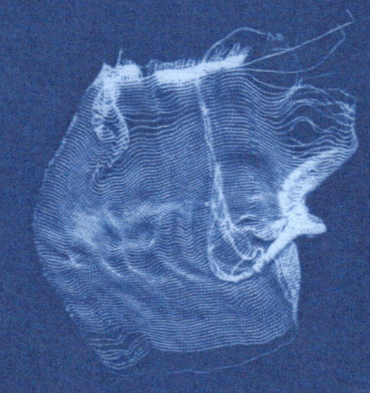

Callithamnion sericus.

Trainer

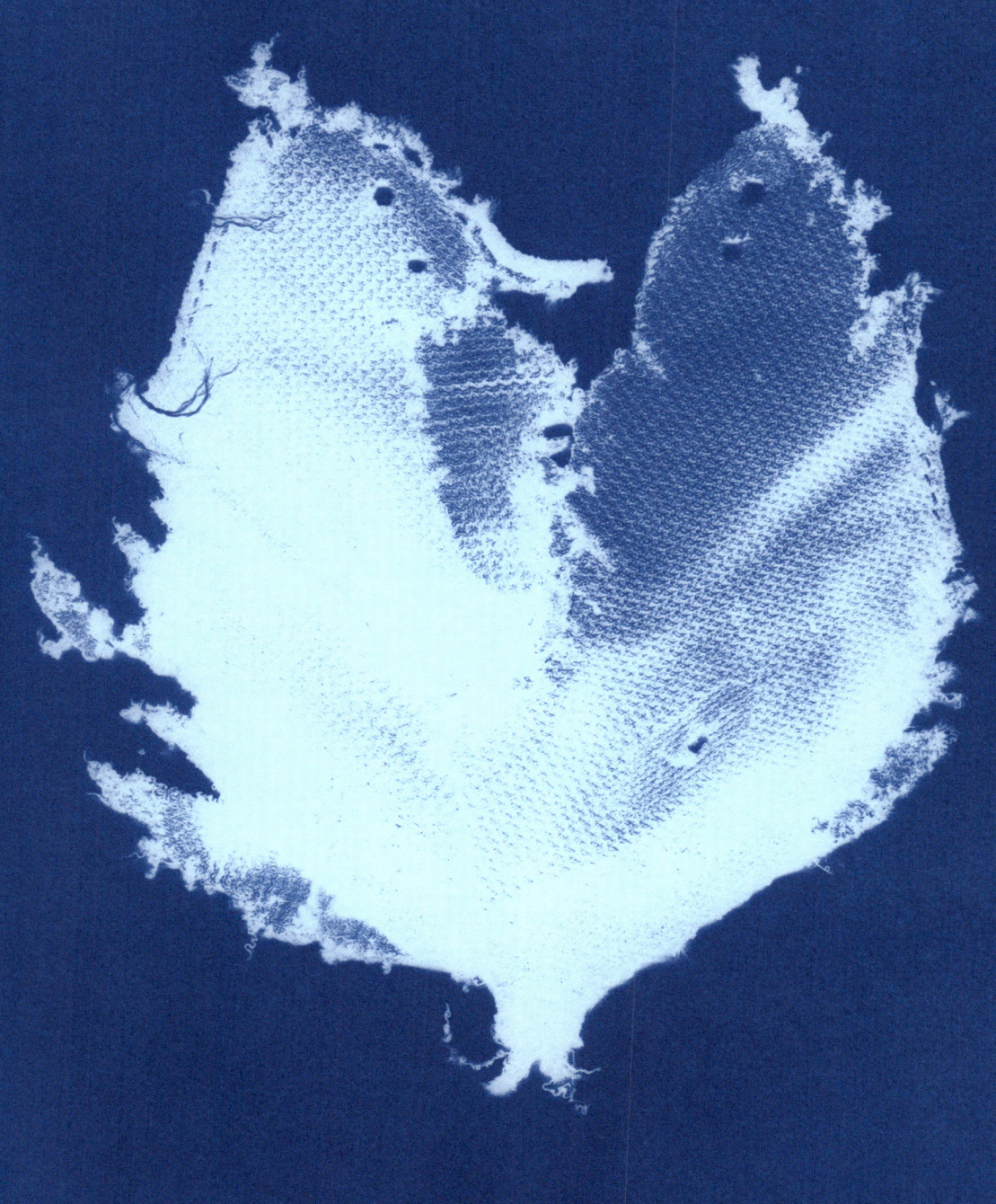

Ectocarpus discipline.

Shoe inside lining

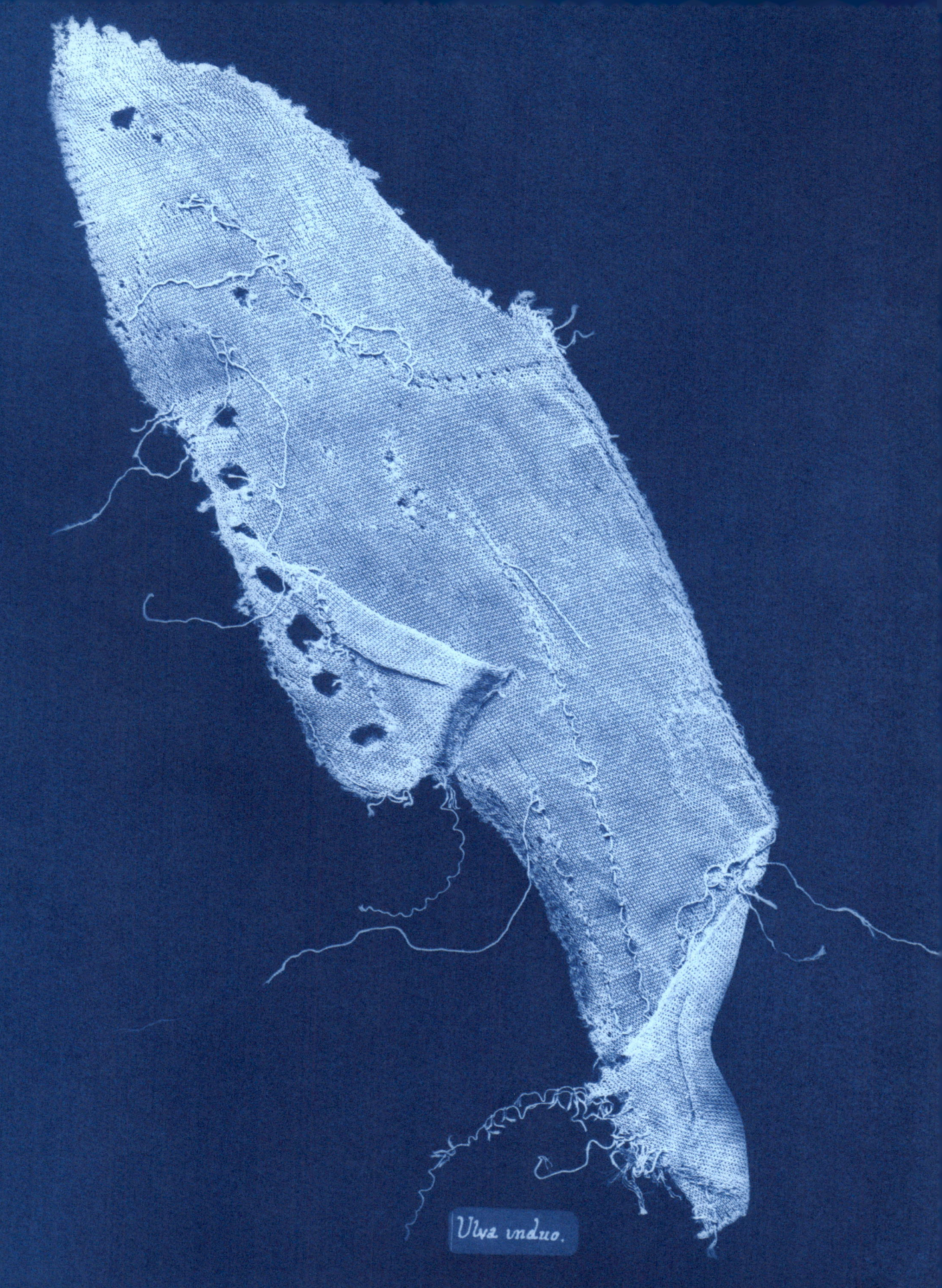

Ulva induo.

Pop sock

Laminaria pedale I.

Sock

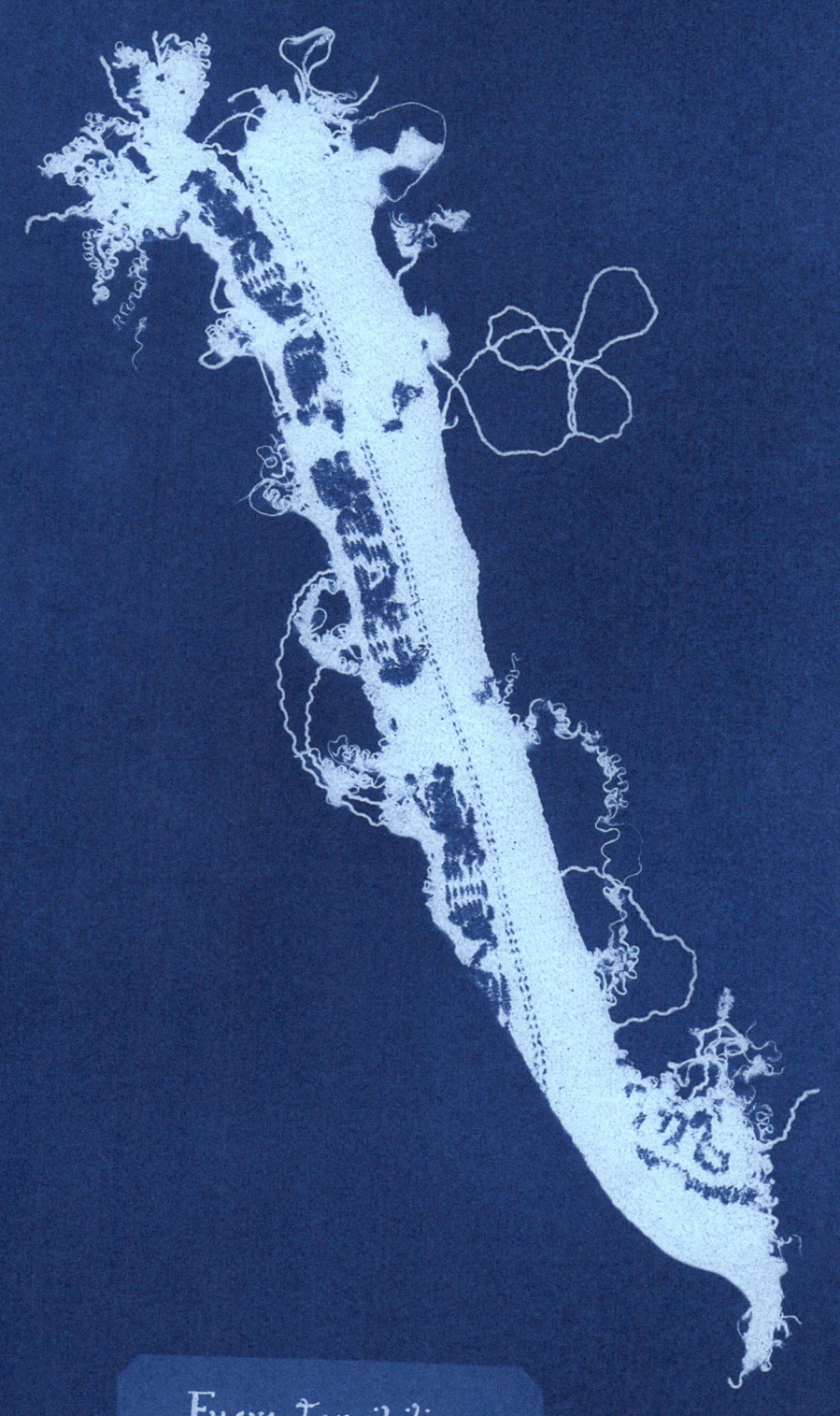

Fucus terribilis.

Nylon tights

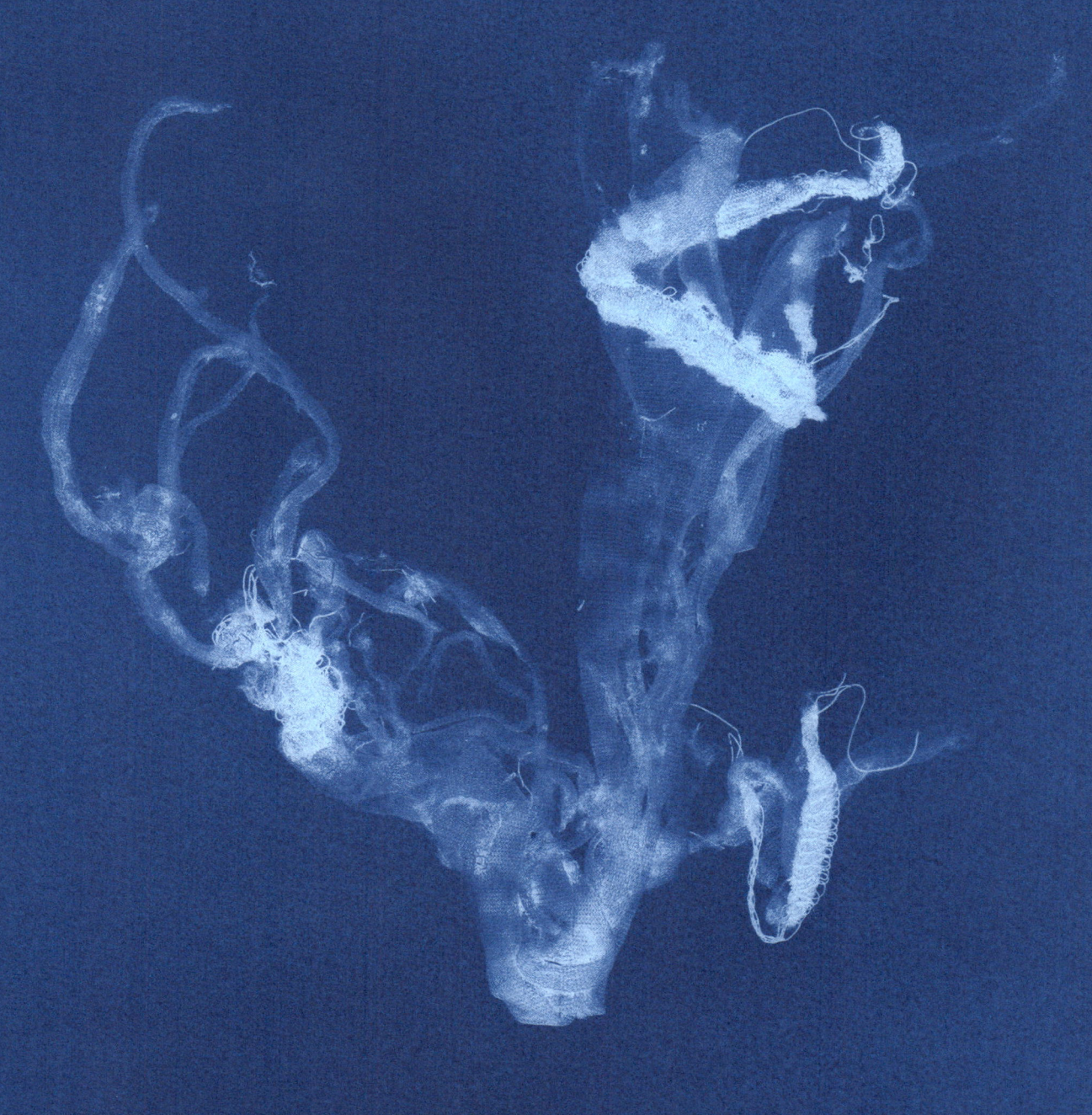

Conferva tibia.

Fishnet tights

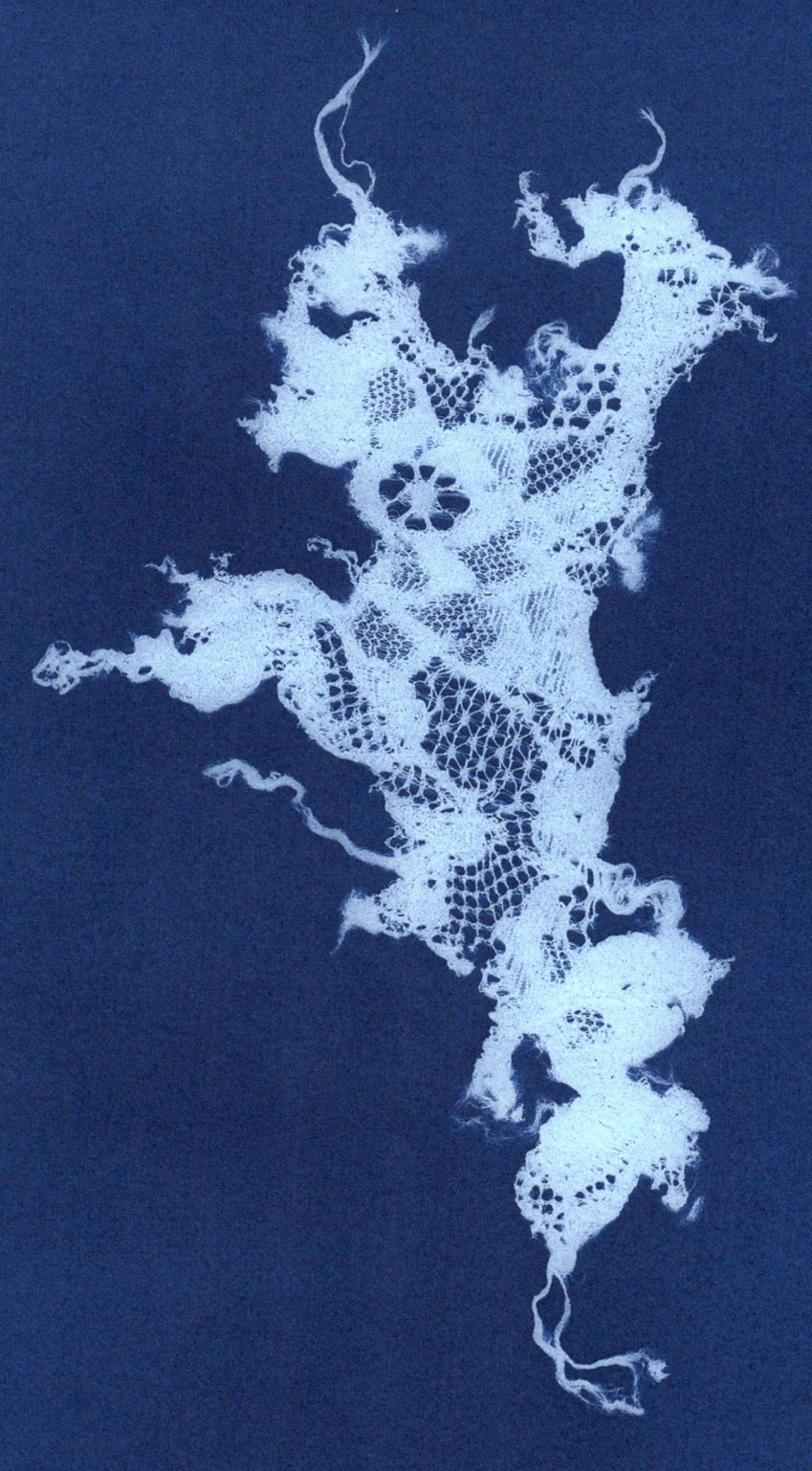

Chylocladia funda

Stocking

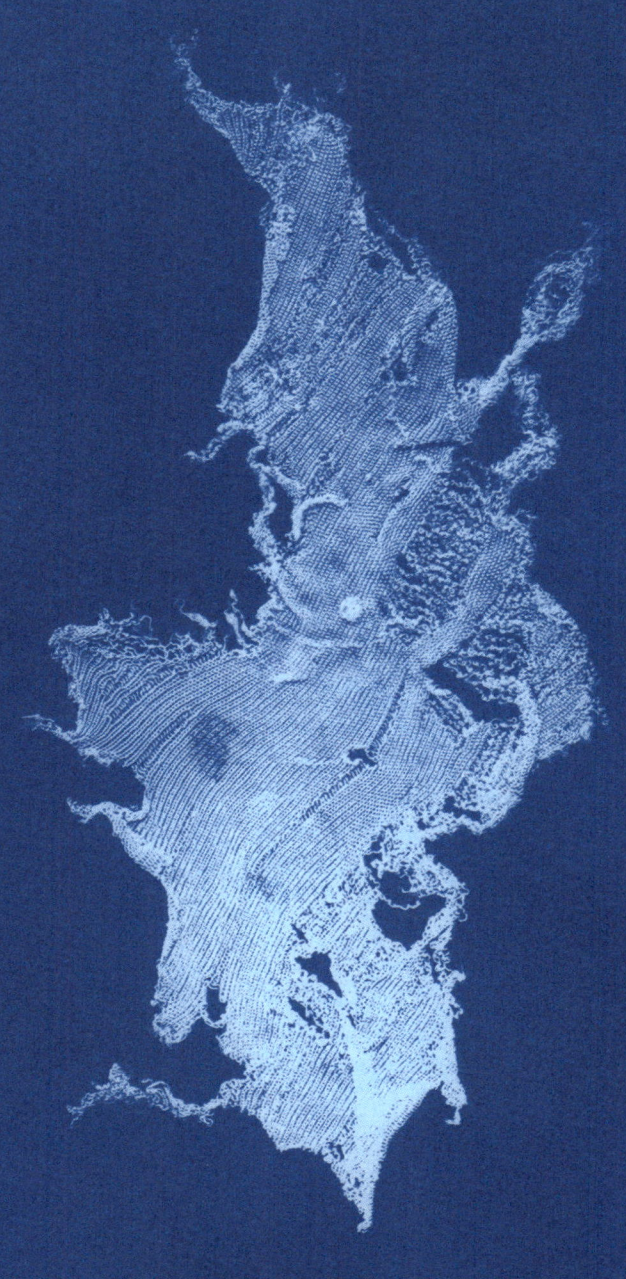

Ectocarpus scalae.

Swim shorts

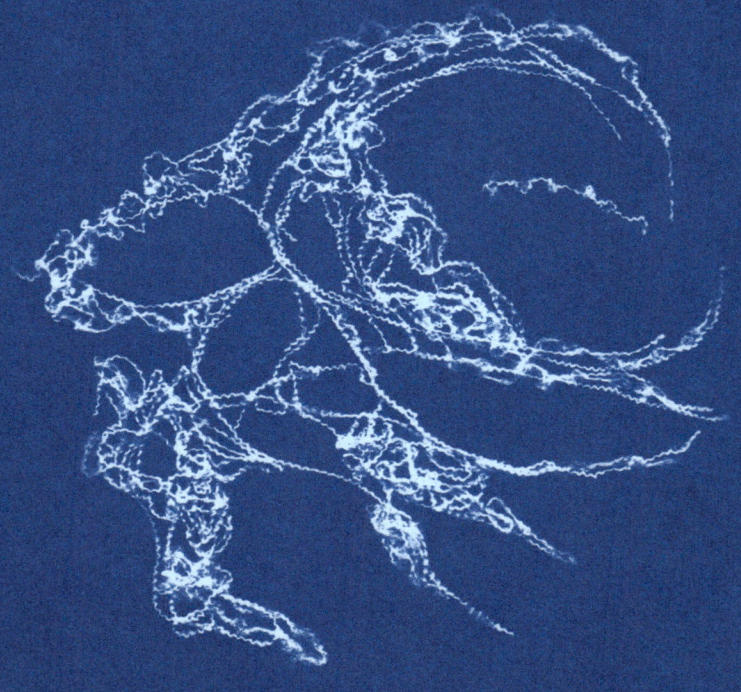

Batrachospermum natare.

Lingerie

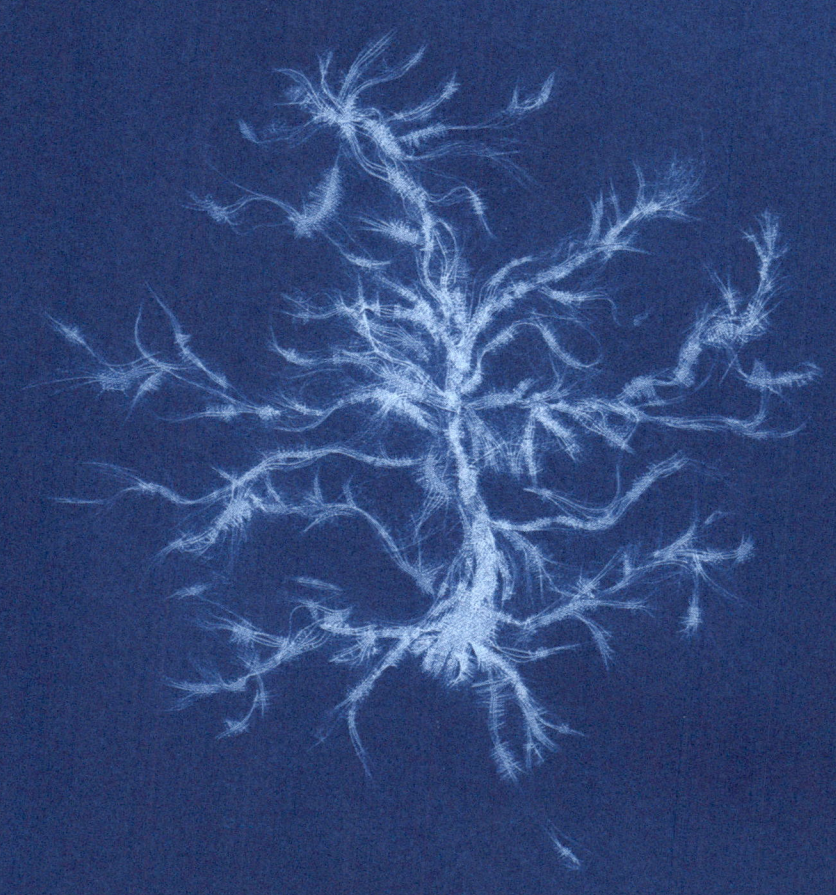

Sphacelaria subter.

Lace camisole

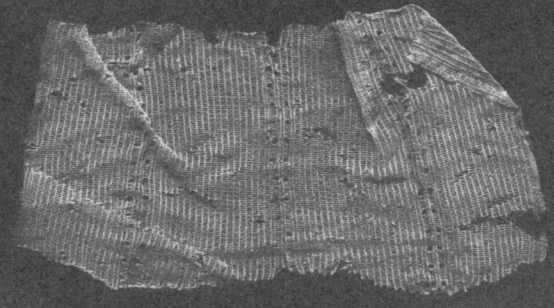

Conferva. subter.
This Conferva, a few years ago
was recovered from the coastal
area of Yorkshire.

Underskirt

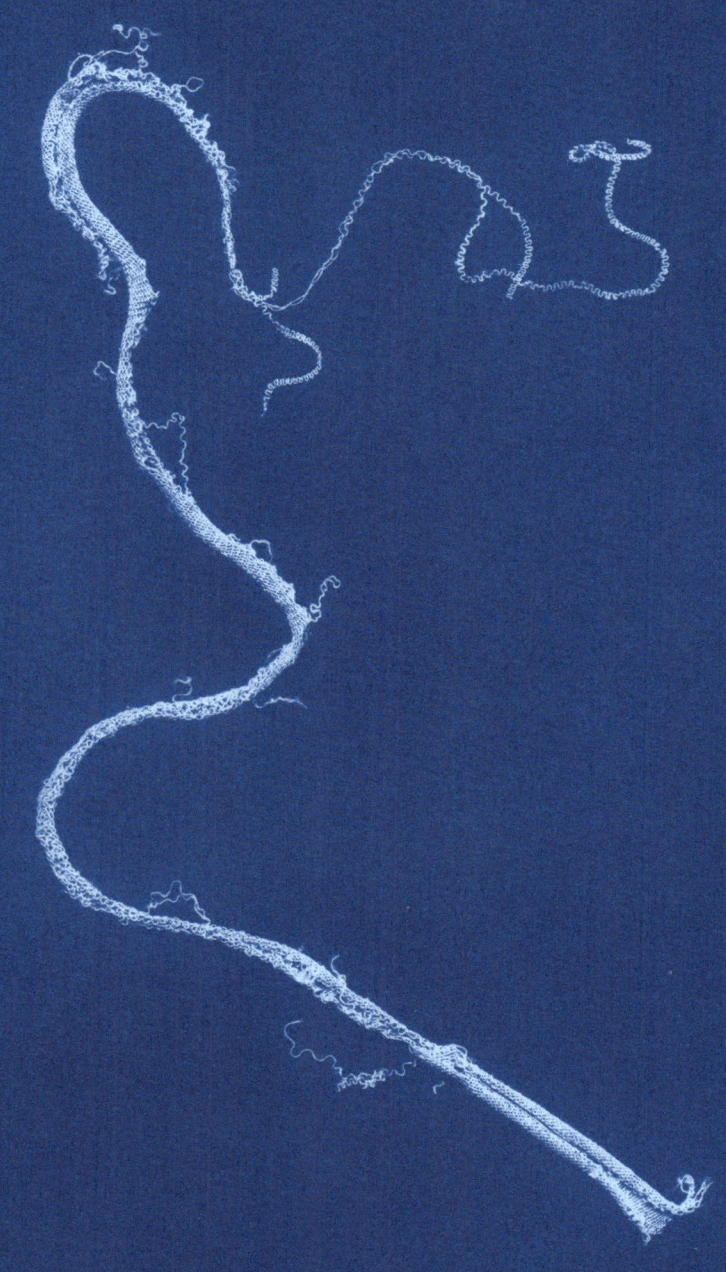

Sporochnus subter
β Vestis.

Petticoat

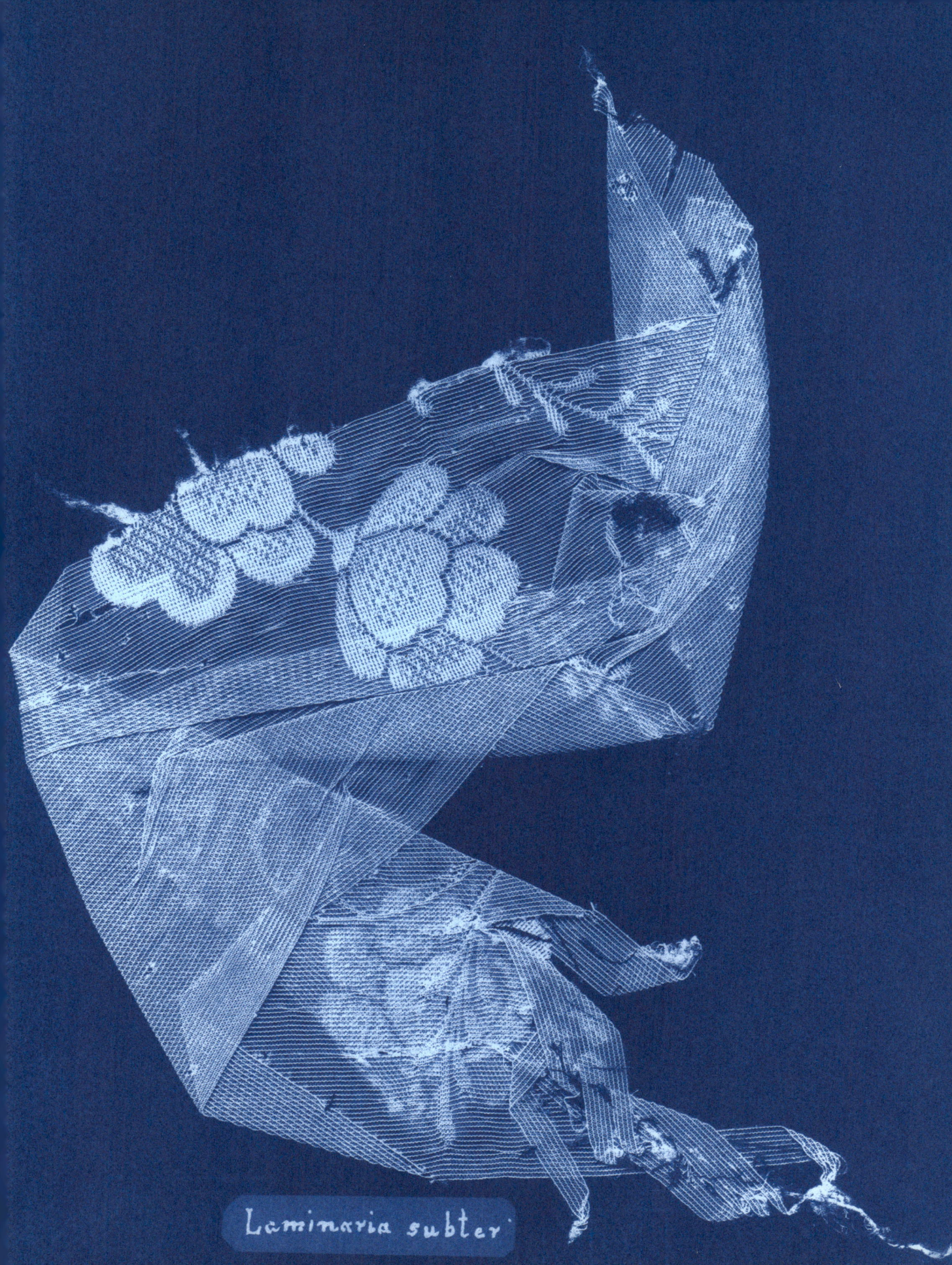

Laminaria subter

Lace knickers

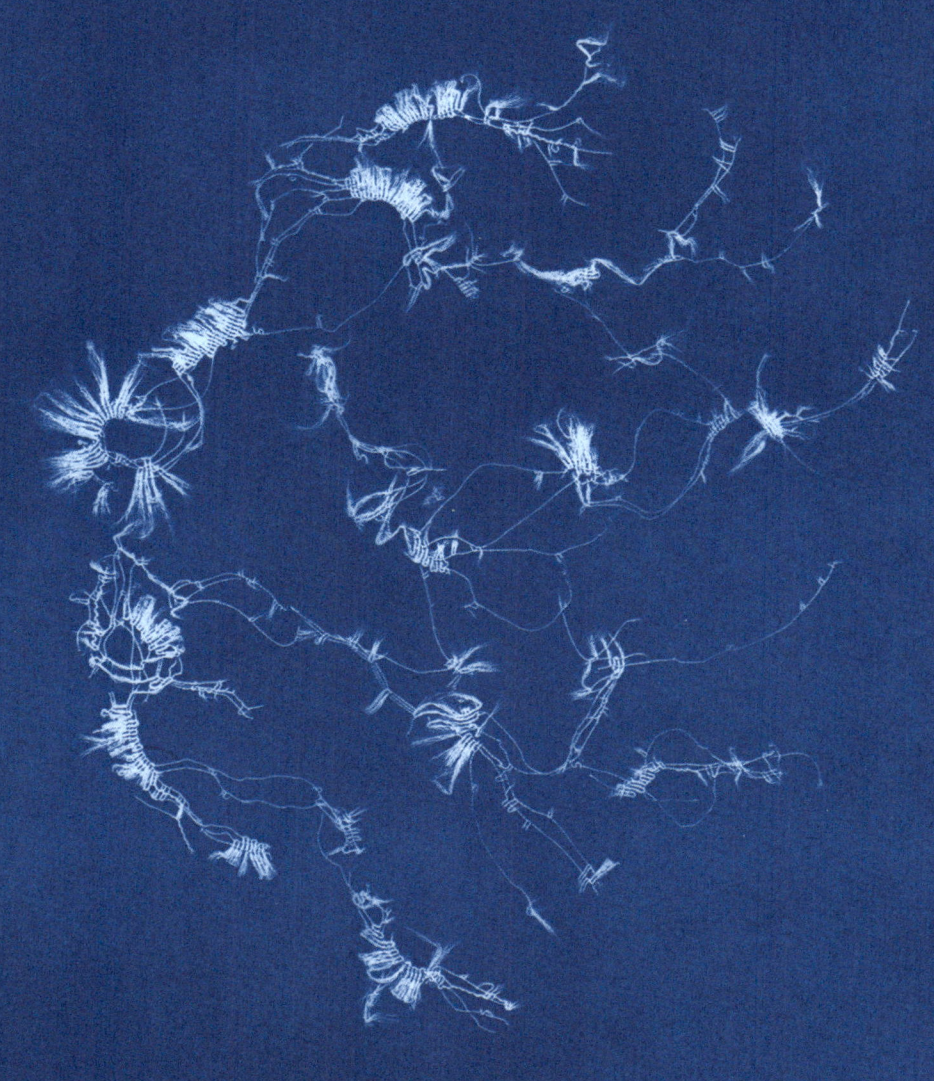

Batrachospermum praetexo.

Knicker elastic

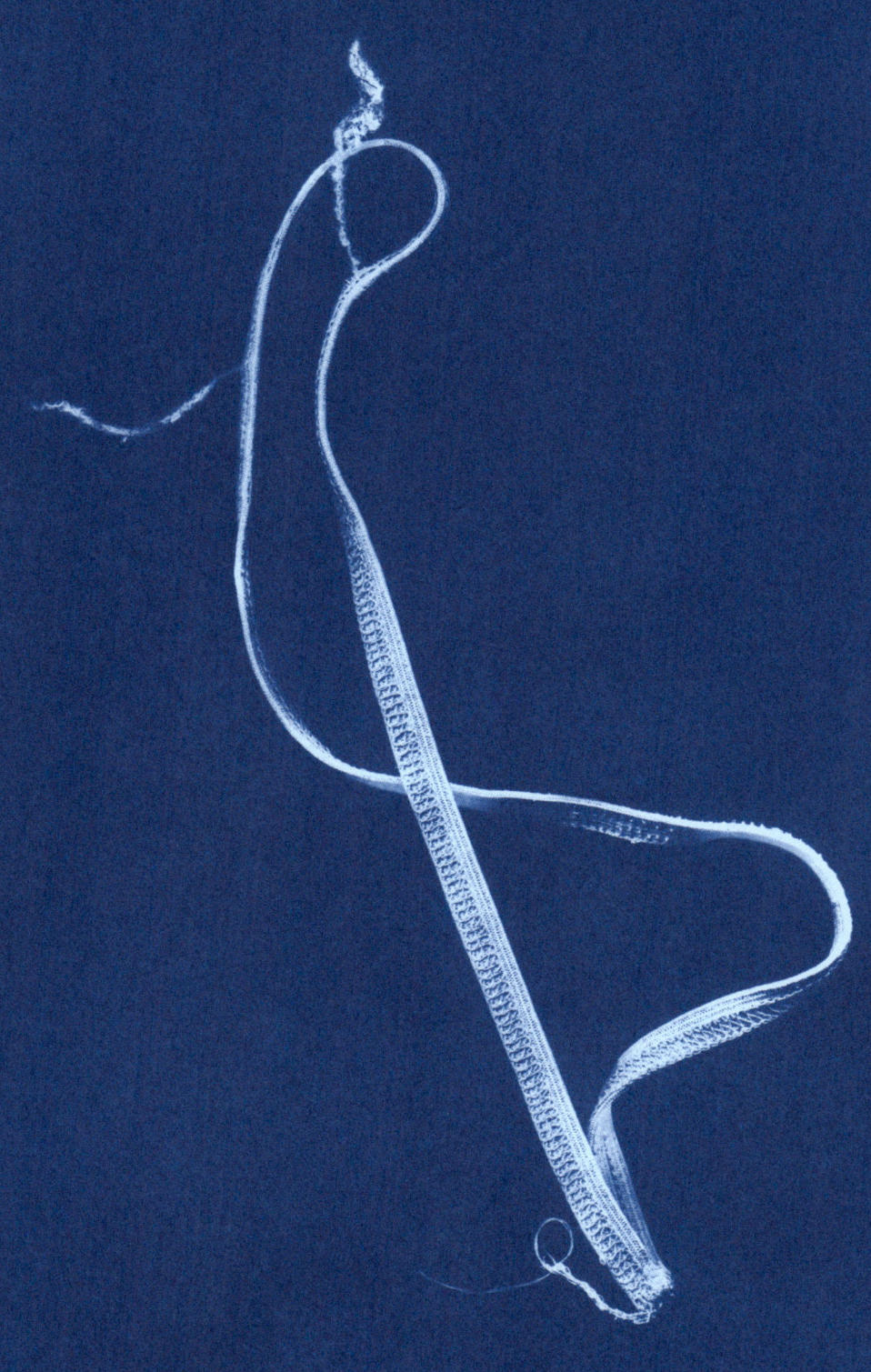

Mesogloia clunis.

Men's underwear

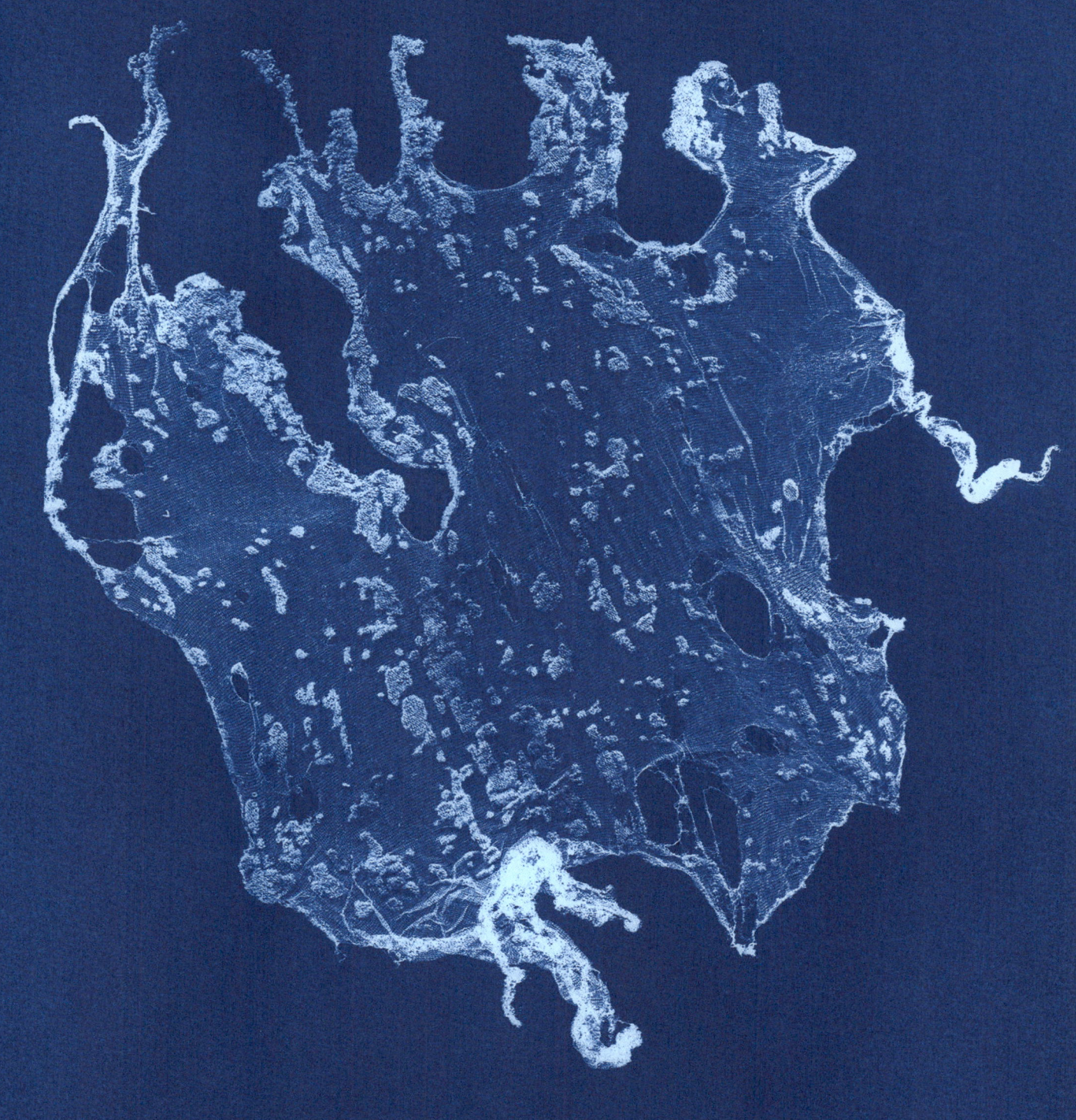

Gigartina ‘y’ frons.

Jersey boxers

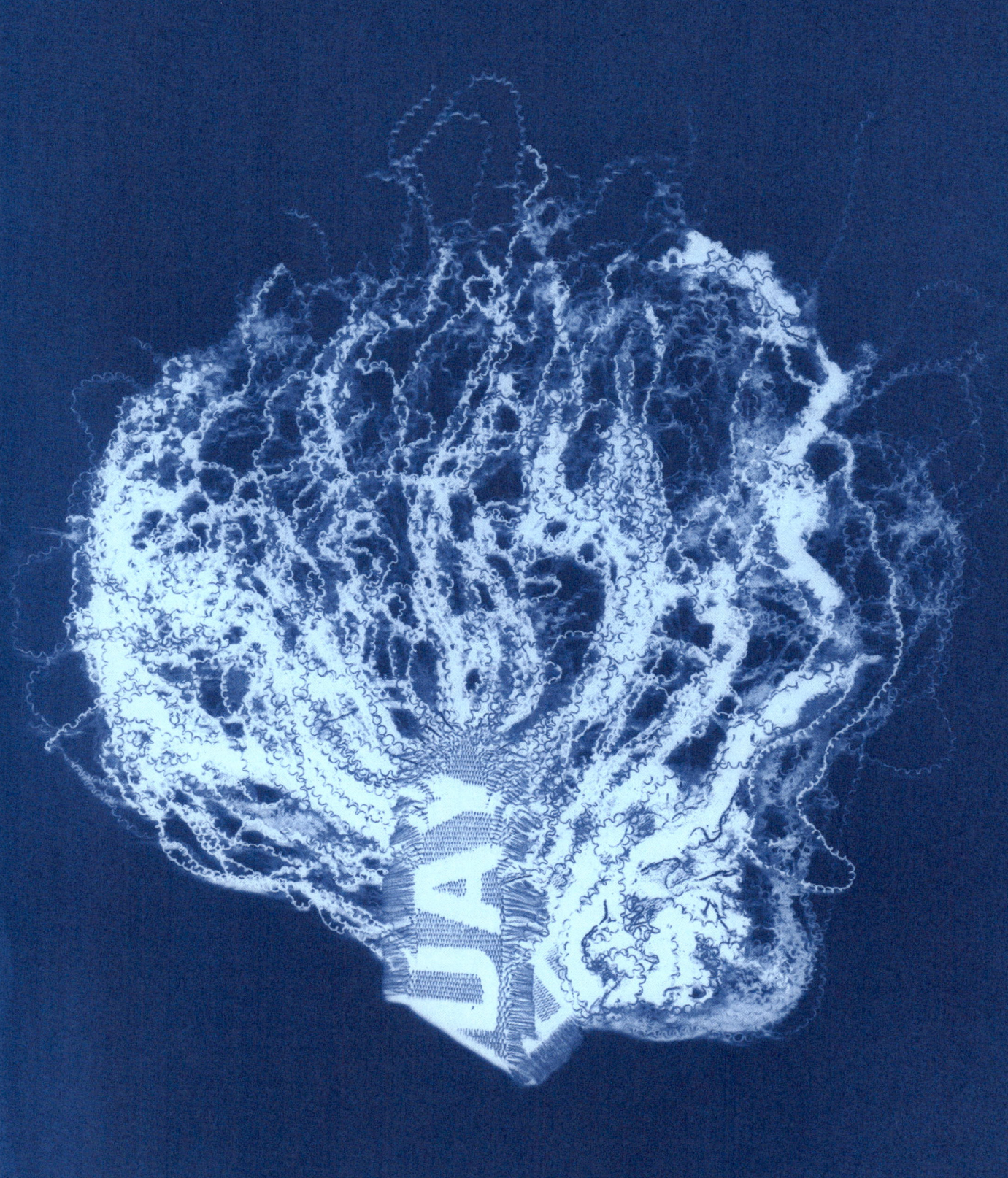

Gigartina sunday.

In 2012, I found a piece of material in a rock pool that changed my life. Mistaking this moving piece of cloth for seaweed, started the recovery of synthetic clothing from around the coastline of Britain for the next ten years.

Photographs of British Algae: Cyanotype Imperfections, aims to raise awareness of fast fashion, synthetic clothes, and the harmful effect of microfibres in the oceans. For the images, I created unique cyanotype prints from clothing that represent the mass consumption and disposal of cheap garments—often worn only a few times—sometimes never at all and then discarded.

Over two hundred 'specimens' of clothing garments recovered from one hundred and twenty-one beaches mimic different species of marine algae. The intention is to engage a wider audience with an issue that is currently having the greatest impact on global climate change. Every year millions of tonnes of clothes are manufactured, worn, and discarded. Clothing from jackets to dressing-up outfits, and football shirts to underwear, were salvaged from beaches, rockpools and directly from the sea, from locations as far north as John O'Groats in Scotland, to Land's End in the South of England. Photograms have been created from this wide range of clothing using the cyanotype process to produce detailed Prussian blueprints, leaving the viewer to contemplate the wearer of these garments before disposal, and of their more recent life in the sea.

The project was inspired by the work of Victorian botanist and photographer, Anna Atkins (British, 1799-1871) who is considered the first person to illustrate a book with photographic images. *Photographs of British Algae: Cyanotype Impressions (1843)*, brought together art and science, illustrated the potential of photography and changed how people looked at science in the 1800s. Seeing the potential to re-create new work in a similar way, I realised I could engage how people view science today, and in connection with the present-day consequences of climate change. My work, *Photographs of British Algae: Cyanotype Imperfections*, reflects the imperfect world of the fashion industry, of mass-produced clothing and of its waste. In the same way that Atkins produced images without using a camera, I present alternative 'specimens' of recovered clothing. Some were created as a direct comparison to Atkins' compositions with synthetic fibres intended to impersonate her original algae, often making it difficult to tell one from the other.

Clothing 'specimens' include complete items of apparel, pieces of material torn and degraded, down to a single stitch or group of microfibres, all selected to show the diversity of clothing waste. Damp clothing was arranged in detailed compositions; some created with the fibres from deconstructed garments, and some left as they were found on the shoreline to form their own arrangements. The clothing was individually pressed and dried in a Victorian cast iron book press to resemble the flat blades and fonds of marine algae. Unlike translucent algae, some of the clothing was often too thick to print from directly and a negative was made to record more detail. When hand-printing the cyanotypes I used the clothing pieces at the same-size and in parallel with Atkins way of working. All specimens were carefully arranged and presented to fit within the page.

To create the images, I applied the cyanotype solution to the paper using the actual pieces of the recovered clothing itself, further connecting the issue to the garment represented. This intention—for the actual cyanotype print to contain microplastic fibres—embeds the idea of the widespread environmental pollution caused by the accumulation of plastic waste, within the print itself, further highlighting clothing waste at sea; it is estimated that 10% of microplastics dispersed in the ocean each year come from textiles.

Each cyanotype print is unique, from the coating of the paper, to the exposure and development—all combining to make a final image that cannot be exactly repeated. Even the paper itself is part of the chemistry, at over one hundred and twenty-five years old, some sheets expose differently due to age, dirt, discolouring, foxing. A crease can create an imperfection. The same original J Whatman paper handmade at the Turkey Mill, Kent, England, as used by Atkins in 1800s, was used for the cyanotype images in this project. Dated and watermarked 1897, it has survived two world wars and was made before the first ever flight—an ironic comparison to the issue it represents now.

Atkins used John Herschel's original cyanotype formula for her prints and whilst this has been used as the basis for my solution, additional elements have been added to create a unique formula for this new work. Some prints have been created by exposing the coated paper to 'artificial' ultraviolet light relating directly to the 'artificial' synthetic plastic specimens portrayed. Other prints were created in the Yorkshire sun, exposed on the hottest days ever recorded in 2022, at 40.3°C (104.5°F), and in 2023 during the hottest year on record, reinforcing the notion of imperfection through climate change, not evident when Atkins created her original 'natural' exposures in the Kent sun in the 1840s.

Captions in the original book were handwritten by Atkins, but for this new work I have re-written the new 'specimens' in the same handwriting style directly on the image. The first word keeps the link to Atkins natural algae, with the second translated to the Latin name of the item of clothing represented. In this publication seventy-four images from a total of 203 have been arranged in specific order throughout the book. Starting with outer garments of clothing, such as a waterproof and parka coat, and ending with inner garments of underwear worn closest to the skin.

I see this book as a discussion point, a call to action, and by publishing the work to circulate and share will reach a wider audience. Whether it ends up on a coffee table, bookshelf, or with someone with the power to implement change, it is my intention that conversation around *Photographs of British Algae: Cyanotype Imperfections* will lead to action and a shift within the fashion industry, with the aim of achieving an impact that will go on to change the world.

To my dearest father.

Quote on page 1 from *International Energy Agency, Energy, climate change and environment: 2016 insights* (2016), p. 113.

The text used in this book is Robert Green's facsimile of the Doves Press typeface, originally cast as a private press font, and eventually thrown into London's River Thames following a business dispute. Many of the original metal type pieces were salvaged decades later and eventually digitaly reconstructed.

Cover: Skivertex® Samala paper, free of harmful plasticisers or heavy metals, FSC™ certified.
Paper: Arena natural rough, FSC™ certified.
Inks: Vegetable based and derived from soy.
Printers: EBS is FSC® certified standards are set in accordance with the requirements of the ISEAL Code of Good Practice for Setting Social and Environmental Standards. This means that the standards are set on the basis of consultations with the major stakeholders. ISEAL is the global association for social and environmental standards systems. FSC® is the only certification scheme in forestry recognised by ISEAL to follow best-practice in standard-setting.

The FSC® logo identifies products which contain wood from forests managed in a correct and responsible manner according to strict environmental, social and economic standards. The forest of origin was checked and evaluated independently in accordance with these standards (principles and criteria of good forest management), established and approved by the participation and consent of the parties concerned.

The FSC® is an international NGO, independent, non-profit organisation that includes among its members, environmental and social groups, indigenous communities, forest owners, industries and trade wood working, scientists and technicians who work together to improve forest management worldwide.

Photographs of British Algae:
Cyanotype Imperfections
First published in 2025
by GOST Books, London

info@gostbooks.com
gostbooks.com

© GOST Books
Images and text © Mandy Barker
mandy-barker.com

Edited and designed by GOST:
Rossella Castello, Katie Clifford, Gemma Gerhard, Justine Hucker, Allon Kaye, Eleanor Macnair, Claudia Paladini, Ana Rocha

Printed in Italy by EBS

British Library cataloguing-in-publication data. A catalogue record of this book is available from the British Library.

ISBN   978-1-915423-79-5

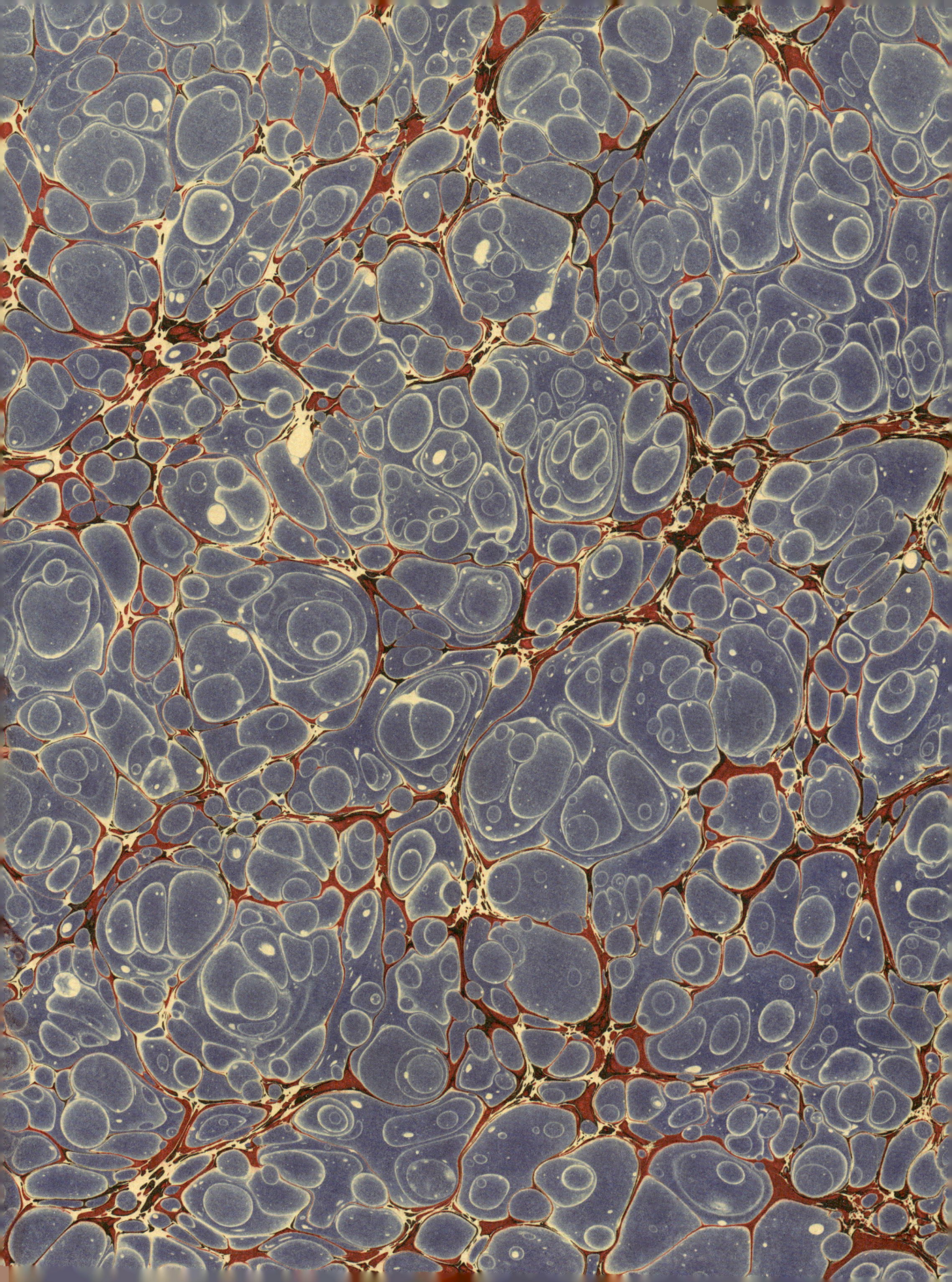

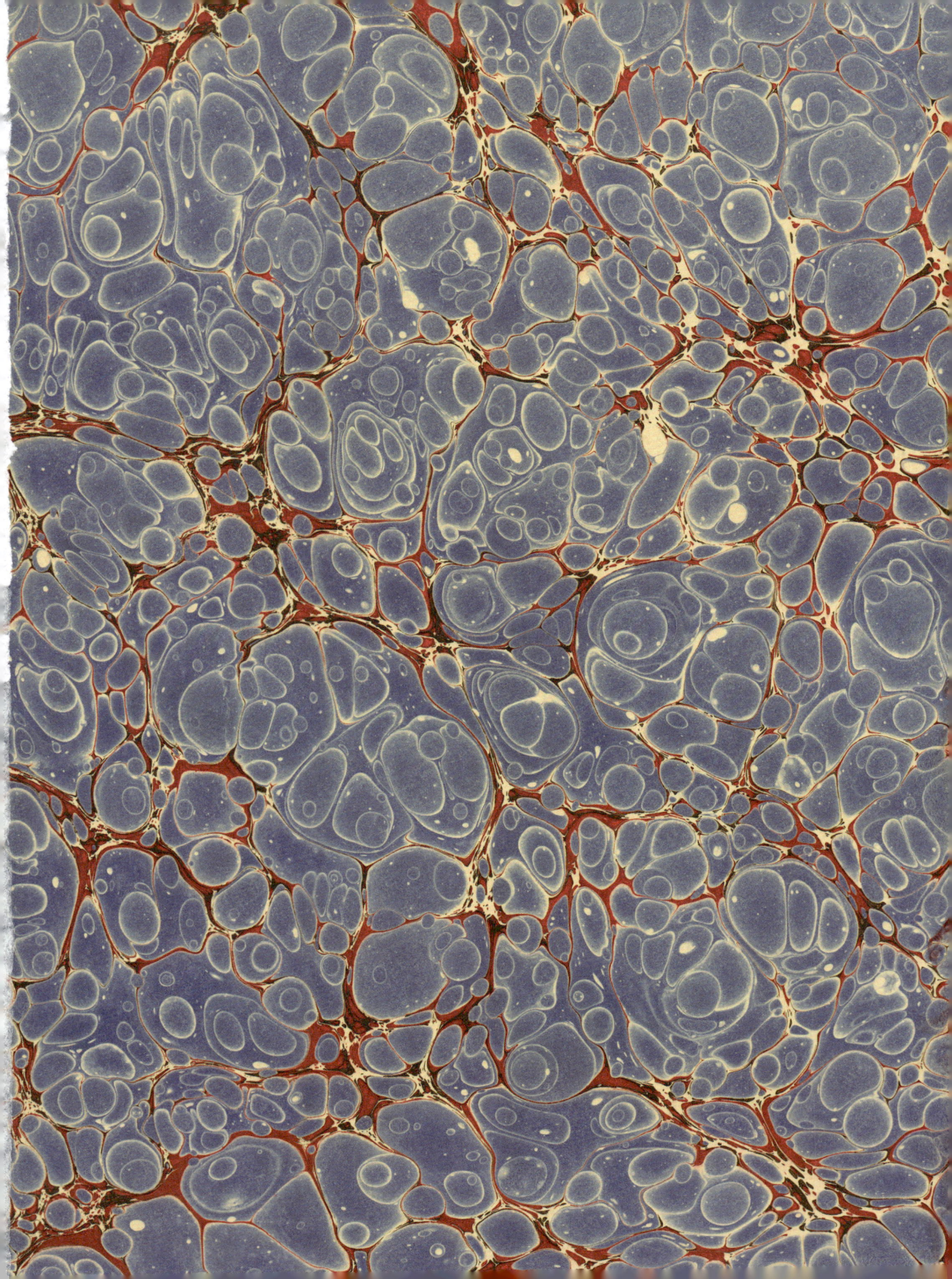